Did Jesus Use A Modem

At The Sermon On The Mount?

Inspirational Thoughts for the Information Age

ELLIS BUSH, JR.

WinePress Publishing
MUKILTEO, WA 98275

Did Jesus Use a Modem at the Sermon on the Mount?

Published by:
WinePress Publishing
PO Box 1406
Mukilteo, WA 98275

Cover by Bill Collier
Illustrations by Glendo Grider

Microsoft and MS-DOS are registered trademarks, and Windows, Word, Windows 95, and Excel are trade-marks of Microsoft Corporation in the United Statesand other countries.

Intel is a registered trademark, and Pentium and Pentium Pro is a trademark of the Intel Corporation in the United States and other countries.

Motorola is a registered trademark in the United States and other countries.

Printed in the United States of America

ISBN 1-57921-066-X
Library of Congress Catalog Card Number: 97-61852

CONTENTS

PREFACE

In the heart of the Glorieta Baptist Conference center is a small lake surrounded by a beautiful chapel, picnic tables, and a miniature golf course. It was while my wife and I were sitting at one of these tables that the idea for this book began. We had just been given the responsibility for teaching a young adult Sunday school class in the small church we attend in central Pennsylvania. We were talking about ways that we could take this class and make it a family. We knew that part of that would include being involved in their daily lives—their lives outside of the church.

As we thought about those in the class, we realized that many of them, like us, either worked for computer companies or used computers in their jobs. Most of them used E-mail addresses as a way to communicate. Why not send out a weekly E-mail to our Sunday school class that would encourage their daily walk with Christ? Why not use a computer analogy to provide a fresh approach to the Christian principles they were living out in their jobs and homes?

The first "Internet Devotional" went out to eight people in my Sunday school class. But the Internet is an interesting method of communication. Once someone receives a message, it is a relatively simple process to take that message and forward it on to another, then to another and another. Each week someone new would send a quick note saying thanks for the devotional and asking to be "put on the distribution list."

Then, in the spring of 1997, these devotionals began appearing on the Daily Wisdom Website, a devotional Website sponsored by Gospel Communications Network (www.gospelcom.net). Since that time, I have had the blessing of hearing from people from all over the world who have read and enjoyed these devotionals. This collection represents the first year of devotionals from Daily Wisdom. I owe a special word of thanks to many of those who have helped make this collection possible:

- Thanks to my young adult Sunday school class, who encouraged me in the initial efforts of these devotionals.

- Thanks to Jo and Warren, who put in many hours managing the Daily Wisdom Website that ministers to thousands of people worldwide.

- Thanks to my men's group. The depth of discussion and challenge in that group is the basis for much of what I write.

- Thanks to Becky, my wife, who has also been my editor, my loving critic, and my patient partner in this endeavor.

- Thanks to God Almighty, from whom all blessings, provision, creative ideas, and loving grace continue to flow each and every day.

In Him,
ELLIS BUSH, JR.
Ellisbush@compuserve.com

vi

DID JESUS USE A MODEM AT THE SERMON ON THE MOUNT?

Did Jesus use a modem,
  At the Sermon on the Mount?
Did He ever try a broadcast fax,
  To send His message out?
Did the disciples carry beepers,
  As they went about their route?
Did Jesus use a modem,
  At the Sermon on the Mount?

Did Paul use a laptop,
  With lots of RAM and ROM?
Were the Epistles posted on a Website,
  At Paul.Rome.Com?
Did the man from Macedonia,
  Send an E-Mail saying "Come"?
Did Paul use a laptop,
  With lots of RAM and ROM?

Did Moses use a joystick,
  At the parting of the Sea?
And a satellite-guided tracking system,

To show him where to be?
Did he write the law on tablets,
Or are they really on CD?
Did Moses use a joystick,
At the parting of the Sea?

Did Jesus really die for us,
One day upon a tree?
Or was it just a Hologram,
Or technical wizardry?
Can you download the live action video clip,
To play on your PC?
Did Jesus really die for us,
One day upon a tree?

Have the wonders of this modern age,
Made you question what is true?
How a single man, in a simple time,
Could offer life anew?
How a sinless life, a cruel death,
Then a glorious life again,
Could offer more to a desperate world,
Than all the inventions of man?

If in your life, the voice of God,
Is sometimes hard to hear.
With all the other voices calling,
His doesn't touch your ear.
Then set aside your laptop and modem,
And all your fancy gear.
And open your Bible, open your heart,
And let your Father draw near.

Interview with an Icon

S o, let me make sure I have this right: You're an Icon.

"Yes, that's right, an Icon. I 'icon' for a living, so to speak."

And basically what is involved in being an Icon?

"To sum up my job in one word: *availability*."

Availability?

"Yes, availability. My job is to wait patiently until needed and to always be available when called upon."

Then when you are called upon, you blossom into some incredible screen with many options and features, right?

"No, not at all. I don't do any of that. In reality, I'm simply a pointer. I point at the software, and the program does all the work—all the fancy stuff. I just point the user toward the software program."

Sounds boring, almost unimportant. You sit there and point.

"Perhaps, but how would anyone get to the program if I were not available to guide them? How would anyone use the software if I were not pointing the way?"

Don't you get frustrated, all that waiting, then your big moment comes, and the software program rushes in and takes all the credit?

"My job could never be frustrating for me, because waiting and pointing was all I was ever designed to do. If I tried to act like the program, I would fail miserably. Truth is, life is pretty good when I relax and do only that which I was created to do: wait and point."

But don't those who use the program often look at you and assume you are the program?

"Yes, and that can be frustrating! I was created as a small image of the program, to represent the program, to point people toward the program. But I am only that—a small picture whose presence on the screen will hopefully attract people to the real program."

And so you wait...

"Yes, and when called upon, I point. Then I wait again. Oh, but while I'm waiting, I often look out from behind my window and watch as the person I pointed toward the program experiences the joy of the program that I pointed them toward. Even my simple life has its wonderful rewards."

Keep yourselves in God's love as you wait for the mercy of our Lord Jesus Christ to bring you to eternal life. Be merciful to those who doubt; snatch others from the fire and save them. (Jude 1:21–23a)

ESCAPE

"No, I'm not quite sure how you got there. Why don't you try the Escape key?"

"It looks pretty messed up to me. Why don't you try the Escape key?"

"No! You don't want to do that! Quick, hit the Escape key!"

The Escape key—that wonderful key whose main function is to get you out of whatever you just got into. I teach computers, and everyday I have a student that somehow, some way, gets into a menu that I have never seen before and have no idea what it does. The menu usually says something like, "Click on OK if you would like to reinstall the entire system at this time," or, "You have accessed a secured government system; any further tampering will cause your location to be bombed."

My advice is always: "Use the Escape key!"

There are times when it is useful to read all the options on a menu and try to figure out how to solve the problem. There are times when it is useful to call the help desk and get some advice from the experts. But there are also times when the best way to handle the problem you have created is to simply use the Escape key.

11

Flee! Run for your lives. (Jeremiah 48:6)

Flee the evil desires of youth, and pursue righteousness, faith, love and peace... (2 Timothy 2:22)

"No, I'm not quite sure how you got there. Why don't you flee?"

"It looks pretty messed up to me. Why don't you flee?"

"No! You don't want to do that! Quick, flee!"

The biblical command to *flee* (or as Monty Python might say: "Run away! Run away!") is a command that is sometimes hard for us proud humans to heed. We feel we know ourselves well enough to know our strengths and our areas of weakness. But God knows us much better than we will ever know ourselves, and He knows the power of fleeing. He knows that fleeing gives us time to think. It gets us out of the middle of a situation and allows us to see things clearly. He realizes that the best way to resist temptation is to avoid temptation. He realizes that some temptations are better to *outrun* than to *outsmart*.

The problem is, we seldom see this for ourselves. We allow ourselves to go deeper and deeper into Satan's territory until all of a sudden we are surrounded, and the human strength we were so proud of is no longer sufficient:

- "I can handle this temptation. I'm strong enough. Don't worry about me, I'll deal with it."
- "It's OK if I spend time with those guys. Their words and actions and attitudes won't rub off on me! Besides, I am supposed to be 'in the world,' right?"
- "Just because I fell into this sin last time doesn't mean I'll fall again! I learned a lot from that experience. I'm ready to take this one head on."

But you, man of God, flee from all this, and pursue righteousness, godliness, faith, love, endurance and gentleness. (1 Timothy 6:11)

The command is simple: Flee. Give it a try this week. When you feel the urge to fight a battle you have had trouble with in the past. When your mind or eyes are tempted to tarry too long where you know they should not be. When you are tired and need a shelter, flee. Then let God refresh you and strengthen you for the battles that He will choose for you to fight.

OLD DISKETTES

I was searching through the storeroom for a new set of whiteboard markers when I stumbled across a box marked 5 1\4-inch diskettes. I thought, *Surely not, we haven't used that type of diskette in several years.* But sure enough, when I opened the box, it was full of brand new, never-been-used, 5 1\4-inch diskettes. When formatted correctly, they can hold 360KB of information! I laughed as I thought about how the large files we create would quickly fill up these old diskettes. Sometimes old tools and old methods of doing things are no longer adequate for the new tasks we must accomplish.

As Jesus was walking beside the Sea of Galilee, he saw two brothers, Simon called Peter and his brother Andrew. They were casting a net into the lake, for they were fishermen. "Come, follow me," Jesus said, "and I will make you fishers of men." At once they left their nets and followed him. (Matthew 4:18–20 NIV)

"…They left their nets…." The nets that had provided their income, their means of support, their financial security. The nets they had used since childhood. These nets felt comfortable in their hands. They knew how to use these nets. They knew their touch and feel. They felt at home when they held these nets.

The nets that had defined who they were in their community, "For they were fishermen." These nets provided a role, a status, a purpose.

But at the call of Jesus, they left their nets " …at once."

They did not take the time to store the nets, so that they might be available for later use. Something in the voice of Christ told them they would never need the nets again.

They did not take the time to sell the nets to help provide for their new ministry. They saw in the eyes of Christ a confidence that assured them—He would be their provision.

They did not try to bring the nets along. Something in the call of Christ said that their new task would require new tools. It was time to leave the nets behind.

They left their nets and followed Him.

Christ still calls people today to follow Him. As a believer, Christ has called you. Where are your nets? Have you left them in the sand, or have you decided to bring them along?

Are you lugging around the nets of provision, trusting in your own ability to provide for your daily needs?

Are you dragging along the nets of talent, offering your skills when Christ wants your heart?

Are you still holding on to the status that your nets once provided, the nets that defined who you were before Christ said, "Come, follow Me"?

Nets can be heavy, can't they? It's hard to carry the Bread of Life when your hands are holding old nets. It's hard to "Go into the all the world," when your feet are tangled in old nets.

At once they left their nets and followed Him.

Leave your nets. Follow Him.

OLD DISKETTES (PART TWO)

I n the back corner of our storeroom was an old box of 5 1\4-inch diskettes. Needless to say, these old diskettes were not of much use on the systems we use today, but I had an idea. The main problem was that these older, larger diskettes would not fit in the newer, smaller diskette drives. After several hours of contemplation, followed by a few minutes of measuring and cutting, I developed a way to modify these old diskettes so that they would fit nicely into the newer diskette drives.

For today's devotional, in addition to the usual spiritual insight, I would like to pass along a practical tip: When you cut an older, larger diskette to allow it to fit in a newer, smaller diskette drive, make certain that you cut it in such a way that the hole remains exactly in the middle. Otherwise, unpredictable results may occur!

The truth is that all the cutting in the world will not let these old diskettes work in new drives. Times change. Systems change. Old diskettes are left behind.

And no one after drinking old wine wants the new, for he says, "The old is better." (Luke 5:39)

17

Old is better? Hold on a minute! Since when was something old better than the newer, faster, better replacement? They can't be serious!

But yet this verse says that the old wine is the good wine. Perhaps this is because the old wine has had years of preparation and care. The old wine is saved for special occasions. The old wine is cherished for its flavor, its fullness.

Is not wisdom found among the aged? Does not long life bring understanding? (Job 12:12)

Rise in the presence of the aged, show respect for the elderly and revere your God.... (Leviticus 19:32)

She is old. She does not move as quickly as she once did. Her voice is not as loud. She sits quietly as the people around her sing. Not because her heart is not singing, but because her eyes can no longer read the words. The tunes are a little too fast. The music is a little too loud. But though her lips are quiet, her heart still rejoices.

He does not say much anymore, and when he does, his speech is slow. But his thoughts are clear and concise. Refined by his years, tested by time, his wisdom is the wisdom that can only come with years. If only we would take the time to listen.

God,

I live in a generation that tells me young is best, youth is to be sought after, old is...old. But there are those around me that have walked with You for twice as long as I have lived. Their hearts have been molded to Your heart, their souls have communed with You more than I can know. And I am ashamed as I see how I have tried to conform them to the "new ways," when I should have been learning from them the value of old wine.

Father, begin in me the long process of preparing me to become a worthy keeper of the old wine. Let me never forget the wisdom, the beauty, and the strength of those who have kept the wine before me. Amen.

OLD DISKETTES (PART THREE)

☙

As we finished cleaning out the storeroom and putting everything back in its place, we finally had to make a decision on what to do with the perfectly good, brand new, 5 1/4-inch diskettes. They had been saved for a reason, but that reason no longer existed. They were still usable, but we did not have a use for them. It would be silly to keep them around any longer; we knew we would never need them.

In the end, we threw them out and wrote them off. We bought them with the best intentions, but to hang on to them now would serve no purpose other than to take up space and make people wonder about our ability to choose office supplies.

And they returned and prepared spices and perfumes. And on the Sabbath they rested according to the commandment. But on the first day of the week, at dawn, they came to the tomb, bringing spices which they had prepared. (Luke 23:56–24:1)

As this Easter season comes to a close, there is one question that is still running through my mind: What happened to the spices? You know, the spices the women prepared and took to the tomb. I read the Scriptures and even did a word search with my on-line concordance, and after the verse quoted above, the spices are never mentioned. The women put a great deal of effort into the spices, which were prepared to anoint the greatest man that ever lived. They were purchased out of love and carried with trembling hands across Jerusalem very early in the morning, then never mentioned again.

Never mentioned because they were never used. Never used because their purpose was no longer necessary. Forgotten because of what they represented: The women had come to the tomb expecting to anoint the dead. Perhaps in their heart they had an unspoken thought that He might be alive, but what they carried in their hands showed what they believed to be true: He was dead. And from that day forward, the only purpose of the spices would be to give evidence of their lack of faith, their lack of belief in what the Savior had told them so many times: "In three days, I'll rise."

My guess is that they left the spices at the tomb. The excitement of the event overtook all those present, and where the spices were or who was watching out for the perfume quickly became irrelevant. The joy of the resurrection overshadowed the presence of the spices and what they represented.

There is a side of me that wonders how the women could show such a lack of faith by carrying burial spices to witness a resurrection. But there is another side of me that understands completely. I look at my own life and, like spices in my hands, I see so many elements of unbelief:

- The efforts I make on my own when I should be taking things to Christ.
- The fear I feel in the night when I should be resting in God's Spirit.
- The stress in the pit of my stomach when I know that Jesus offers peace and stillness.

Above all, Easter is a season of resurrection. A season of renewal. A season of starting over. Let this be true in our lives as well. Let this be a season when we ask God to show us the areas of unbelief in our own lives. Then pray that He will give us the strength to leave these areas at the tomb, forgotten and unneeded because of the resurrection of our Lord.

He is risen! He is risen, indeed!

BIBLICAL TRADITIONS
REGARDING WINDOWS

Then Noah decided to check and see if there was dry land. He fired up his laptop computer, which seemed to take forever to boot-up and finally, "After forty days, Noah opened the window he had made" (Genesis 8:6). He was very frustrated that it took him forty days to open the window, but he was only using a 286 with 640KB of RAM, so what could he realistically expect?

Like Noah, others were also disappointed by early versions of Windows. In 1 Samuel 19:12, it is recorded that David was let down by a window, and he fled and escaped. (Who among us has not been let down by Windows on occasion.)

You can almost hear excitement turn to disappointment in the young woman's voice when she exclaims, "My lover is like a gazelle or a young stag. Look! There he stands behind our wall.…" Then she realizes that he is distracted by his new Pentium system and she continues, dejected: "scrolling through the windows" (Song of Solomon 2:9; paraphrased).

Early computer viruses were often referenced. For example, Jeremiah warns that "death has climbed in through our windows…" (Jeremiah 9:21). In later verses he attributes this to a woeful lack of pre-release testing. (Note: Some manuscripts omit these verses to avoid legal reprisals.)

Others had more success at using their systems. Elisha "opened the east window" (2 Kings 13:17), and Jeremiah was renowned throughout the land, because "he makes large windows" (Jeremiah 22:14) and was able to use the tile facility so that "the windows were placed high, in sets of three" (1 Kings 7:4). Using the color feature, he was able to make them "with cedar and decorated in red."

However, most of the Old Testament Windows users were not very productive, because there was nothing in their Windows until several thousand years later, when Paul "shook the dust from his feet in protest and went to Iconium" (Acts 13:51), where first-century "icons" were created. But even Paul himself had difficulty with the new systems. He was later put in prison because one of the icons, named Eucalyptus, fell out of the window and was "picked-up dead" (Acts 20:9), which is not a good thing.

And finally, I would be remiss if I did not point out that the Bible also speaks to the future of Windows. How telling are the verses in Ecclesiastes 12:3–5, where the writer predicts: "The keepers of the house tremble, and the strong men stoop and those *working with windows grow dim*.…Then man goes to his eternal home and mourners go about the streets" (author's emphasis).

Some scholars see this as predicting that Windows will be the death of us all, but the original text is unclear on this. Some think that the reference to "grow dim" is referring to mental capability, not physical demise. I think both translations have an element of truth.

Our mouths were filled with laughter… (Psalms 126:2)

"GoTo" Therefore
and Teach...

In most Windows applications, there is a function called the "GoTo" function. This allows you to move from where you are, to another place in the application that you are working on. In Microsoft Word, you can simply hold down the CTRL key and hit the G, and this will present the GoTo menu. The nice thing about this menu is its simplicity. You choose the GoTo option and it asks, "Where do you want me to go?" There are no other options, no debates on where the best place to go might be, no suggestions on where you might really want to go. The system just asks: "To where?"

It's hard to describe the GoTo function in each of our lives, but when God selects that function, we usually know it. It happens when a small voice inside says: "There's somewhere I'd like you to go for Me. There's a purpose I need to accomplish and it involves you."

Our problem is that when we see the GoTo menu pop up in our lives, we immediately assume it means: "GoTo Asia, live in a grass hut, and translate the Scriptures into Sanskrit." Or worse yet: "GoTo the person in the next cubical, tell them they're a sinner, lay hands on them, and speak in Sanskrit." And so we use one of the most accessible keys on the keyboard—the Escape key.

Have you noticed what happens when the GoTo menu pops up on your screen and then you hit the Escape key? The menu goes away. What could be easier? We didn't want to go anywhere anyway. So that takes care of that. The menu is gone and so is the GoTo request. But is this the best way to respond to God's GoTo?

God used a bright light to issue a GoTo command to Paul. In Acts 22:10, his response was simply, "What Shall I do, Lord?"

An angel named Gabriel (which is the Greek word for GoTo) came to Mary with news that she would bear the Messiah, and she responded, "Be it done according to your word."

The GoTo menu popped up in their lives, and their response was simply, "To where?" No excuses, no questioning, no Escape key. Just a willingness to go and a faith that the God who issued the command would be faithful to sustain them, wherever He might lead.

So what have the GoTo's sounded like in your life recently? "GoTo that person in the next office and ask them how their day is going?" Or, "GoTo lunch with the other folk in the project you're working on and find out what's on their mind? Or, "Get out of bed and GoTo church!" Or perhaps even, "Go To Asia, live in a grass hut, and translate the Scriptures into Sanskrit."

Make a decision today to listen for God's GoTo's in your life. And commit ahead of time to respond by saying, "To where?" To whatever destination our sovereign and loving God has for your life.

THE LANGUAGE OF LOVE

And then the programmers came to Jesus and asked, "Master, which is the greatest language of them all?"

And Jesus responded saying, "The greatest language is the language of Love."

And the programmers scoffed and bickered among themselves, because they had never heard of this language. They had used Cobol and Fortran and even PowerBuilder and did not see how a language they had never used could be better than all the languages that they had studied all their lives.

So they confronted Jesus in an effort to trick Him and asked, "In this new language called *Love*, what are the most powerful commands available to you?"

And Jesus answered saying, "The language has but two commands: Love God and love man."

And the programmers were further incensed and proclaimed to each other, "Perhaps he has developed a new RISC system with an instruction set of two? But how can these two instructions that we have never used before be so much better than all of the instructions we have spent our lives learning and use everyday?"

And so they confronted Jesus again and said, "How is it that your two-instruction language can be so powerful? Our languages have many instructions, with many variables associated with each instruction. The more instructions available, the more combinations of instructions you can create and the more you can accomplish. What can you accomplish with only these two commands?"

Then Jesus asked the programmers, "If a man truly loves God with all his heart and soul and mind, and truly loves his brother as much as he loves himself, is there anything that such a man cannot accomplish?"

And the programmers were perplexed and confused because they had never thought of it that way before. As the programmers continued to debate and discuss these issues, Jesus asked, "Are there those among you who would like to learn this new language called Love."

And one programmer spoke right up saying, "What is the training schedule for this language? Surely with only two commands, we can learn this language in a matter of weeks, or with off-site training, only a few days!"

But Jesus responded, "I can place the basic principles of this language into your life in the blink of an eye, but to master the language will take you a lifetime."

And a great uproar was heard among the programmers because these were bright programmers who could master any set of commands in a short amount of time. The roar turned to laughter as they joked about how foolish anyone would be to start learning a language that took so long to master. Then they slapped each other on the back and strolled back to their cubicles, knowing that this language must not be for real; or if it was for real, it was not for them. (Based on Matthew 22:34–46; paraphrased.)

UNDO

There is a small island in Indonesia called Sumba. On the eastern coast of this island there is an area called the Tanjung Undu, which in English means, "The Land of the Undo People." After extensive research on this area, I have decided that this is where I would like to live. Due to an atmospheric anomaly and the way the rotation of the earth affects that part of the world, the people of this region have been gifted with a genetic Undo function that allows them to quickly and easily take back the last thing they have said without anyone knowing that it was ever said.

- A husband speaks harshly to his wife. No harm done, just use the Undo function.
- Two neighbors gossip about what the pastor's wife was wearing on Sunday. No sin is committed, just use the Undo function.
- A word is spoken in anger between two lifelong friends. No relationship is broken, just use the Undo function.

But no one can tame the tongue; it is a restless evil, and full of deadly poison. (James 3:8)

The gift of communication is perhaps one of God's dearest gifts to us. Using simple words, we can express love, gratitude, honor, and many other positive emotions that we feel for others. But words can also express pride, fear, distrust, and other negative emotions that we struggle with each day.

And be kind to one another, tender-hearted, forgiving each other, just as God in Christ also has forgiven you. (Ephesians 4:32)

While God did not create an Undo function for the words we say, He did create the *repentance* and *forgiveness* function. And perhaps more than any other function, it is this ability to ask for and receive forgiveness from others that holds the Body of Christ together. It is one of the central functions that separate us from the world around us. And, unfortunately, it is a function that we do not use enough.

Perhaps what keeps us from asking for forgiveness is fear that our brother will not receive our repentance. Perhaps a hardened life keeps us from forgiving someone. Perhaps it is weariness that keeps us from opening up our lives one more time to those who have hurt us or whom we have hurt, and beginning the long, sometimes difficult, process of restoration.

I entreat you to walk in a manner worthy of the calling with which you have been called, with all humility and gentleness, with patience, showing forbearance to one another in love, being diligent to preserve the unity of the Spirit in the bond of peace. (Ephesians 4:1–3)

While there is a place called Tanjung Undu on the east coast of Sumba, in reality, the people who live there struggle with the problems their words create, just as we do. And as nice as it might be to have an Undo function to correct the things we have said and done, the odds are unlikely that scientists will develop this in our lifetime.

Fortunately, God has shown us how to repent and re-store. So as you use the Undo function on your computer this week, let it serve as a reminder to repent of the harm-ful words you have spoken and a reminder to forgive the words that have been spoken against you.

The 23rd Psalm
(With Confessions from a Computer User)

The Lord is my Shepherd,
I shall not want.

But Lord, I do want. I want a Pentium processor, with a 300 MHz Chip, CD-ROM, and a 17-inch screen. I want a better job with more pay and a nicer boss. I want a spouse who understands me, kids who listen to me, and a friend with whom I can talk. Lord, I do want....

He maketh me lie down in green pastures,
He leadeth me beside still waters.
He restoreth my soul.

Well, that sounds nice, but who has the time to lie around in a field somewhere. Surely there are other ways to restore my soul. Perhaps I could download this "restoreth" stuff from the internet. At 56,000 BPS, You could restore me in no time.

He leads me in the paths of righteousness,
For His name's sake.

Now I think I understand. I can be restored by editing my CONFIG.SYS to set up my path to look into the righteousness subdirectory. Then I can execute the download...

Yea, Though I walk through the valley of the shadow of death.

Hold on right there. It seems like your map is a little off. How can the paths of righteousness lead me into the valley of death? The restoring part sounded pretty good, but this shadow of death stuff isn't exactly what I bargained for...

I shall fear no evil, for Thou art with me.
Thy rod and thy staff, they comfort me.

But I do fear evil. I fear my health might fail. I might lose my job. If I keep working the hours I've been lately, I might lose my wife. I guess You're right: with fears like these, I must already be in the valley of the shadows. Perhaps some of the comfort I need could be found by those still waters after all. God, you know how stubborn I am. If it's necessary, use that rod and staff to point me in the right direction.

Thou preparest a table before me,
In the presence of mine enemies.
Thou hast anointed my head with oil.
My cup overflows.

Wow, overflows? Really? When You restore, You must really do it right. And even in the presence of my enemies, boy that will make them jealous.... Oh, sorry, I guess they need some of this comfort, too. Perhaps that's where some of my overflow needs to flow. (And by the way, my hair is already a little too oily. So go easy on that part, if you would.)

Surely goodness and mercy shall follow me all the days of my life.

And I shall dwell in the house of the Lord forever. Amen.

Lord, I do want. And I do fear. And I don't like mine enemies. And I'm scared of the valley of death. But my prayer is that You would replace all of these with the knowledge that Your goodness, and Your mercy and Your grace are with me forever. And starting even now, I can live in Your presence forever. Thanks, and Amen.

Recognized Voices

This new program was great! All I had to do was talk to the computer and it immediately typed on the screen exactly what I was saying…almost.

I said, "Blessed are the poor in Spirit."

The computer typed: Breathless are the four who spear it.

I said, "The meek shall inherit the earth."

The computer typed: The geek's mail is inherently mirth.

And on and on goes my experience with this great new Voice Recognition System. The advertisement said the software would recognize my voice after only a few hours of "teaching" the computer the sound and tone of my voice. So far, I'm not impressed.

The watchman opens the gate for him, and the sheep listen to his voice. He calls his own sheep by name and leads them out. When he has brought out all his own, he goes on ahead of them, and his sheep follow him because they know his voice. (John 10:3–4)

The scene was chaotic: Hundreds of sheep were gathered in the holding pen outside the corral, where the spring sheepshearing was to take place. The shepherds had brought their sheep from all over the surrounding countryside and gathered them together in the holding pen. The time came to begin the shearing process, and the first shepherd simply stepped into the corral and called for his sheep. From the hundreds of sheep there, only a few dozen came forward. Only the ones that belonged to that shepherd, only the ones that recognized his voice.

The scene was chaotic: Thousands of people were hurrying through their lives—fish to be caught, taxes to be collected, Romans to be subverted, lives to be lived. People from every walk of life focused on earning their next meal or building their next barn. Then a Shepherd stepped into the crowd and called out. From the thousands of people there, only a few came forward. Only the ones that desired to belong to the Shepherd came, only the ones that recognized His voice.

The scene is still chaotic: Millions of people hurrying through their lives—meetings to attend, plans to be made, vacations to be enjoyed, lives to be lived. People chasing their goals and dreams. The shepherd continues to call out. From the millions, still only a few come forward. Only the ones that recognize His voice.

My sheep listen to my voice; I know them, and they follow me.

God's voice, like the kind and caring voice of a loving shepherd, is calling you to a deeper knowledge of Him today. Pause for a moment and listen, then follow our Shepherd.

FOLLOWING COMMANDS

The program had compiled successfully and was expected to run without any problems. After executing for several minutes, a window popped-up on the screen with a message from the program: "Excuse me, but do you really want me to do this forecast using polynomial-based mathematical calculations?"

A little taken back, I responded, "Well, yes. That is why I used that command. I need it done using that type of math."

"Well, OK."

And the program continued. Shortly thereafter, it said, "Now about this 'Do Until' subroutine, do you actually want me to continue doing this until you tell me to do something else? I might end up doing this forever!"

"Yes, I need you to follow that command until I give you further instructions. I'll know when it is time to take the next step, and I'll let you know when that time comes. "Well, OK."

And the Program continued. Shortly thereafter, the program ended much sooner than expected. I checked the program output. Confused, I asked, "Why did you stop? There was more to be done."

"Well, I looked over all the commands you gave me and decided to just do the easy ones and skip all the hard ones."

"But why? You are capable of completing all the commands I gave you. I know how you work. I would never give you a command that you could not complete or that was too hard."

"I guess that's true, but I wasn't sure why you wanted me to execute certain commands, and I didn't understand what the overall point of the program was, so I decided to just run myself my way. I guess I just didn't trust you...."

This is love for God: to obey His commands. And His commands are not burdensome. (1 John 5:3)

And this is His command: to believe in the name of His Son, Jesus Christ, and to love one another as He commanded us. (1 John 3:23)

Touch Sensitive

I had spent years learning to type on a keyboard that was admittedly created to keep people from typing quickly. Then I spent months trying to master the fine art of mouse-wrangling. (It took me two days to realize that you had to leave the mouse on the mouse pad and not wave it around in the air like a remote control.)

Now I stood in front of a screen with no keyboard and no mouse but with lots of information that I needed. Finally, as if sensing my confusion, a small message popped-up and instructed me: "Touch the picture to retrieve information about the item."

Touch it? Touch the screen? This was a little odd. But I gave it a try, and sure enough the computer quickly provided the information I needed. I still have not figured out how the touch screen actually works, but the message was clear: If I wanted to communicate with that system, I needed to do so in a way that it would recognize.

After He took him [the deaf and mute man] aside, away from the crowd, Jesus put his fingers into the man's ears, then he spit and touched the man's tongue. (Mark 7:33)

39

We do not know much about the man. He is described as deaf and mute. He was brought to Jesus by some friends who asked Jesus to heal him. And Jesus did, in what I have always thought was a strange and somewhat disgusting way: He poked his fingers in the man's ears and then wiped his spit on the man's tongue!

To the cripple he said, "Arise!"

To the leper he commanded, "Be clean!"

To the bleeding woman, he said, "Your faith has made you whole."

But for the deaf-and-mute man, he poked and spat. Yuck!

They came to my class together, one was hearing impaired, the other a sign-language interpreter. As I taught that day, I also learned. I saw the skill and beauty of the interpreter as she took my spoken words and translated them into signs and expressions that the student could use and understand.

During a break, I let the interpreter know how impressed I was with her ability. She said that this session was not nearly as difficult as when she interprets for someone who is both deaf and blind. When I asked why, she responded that when someone is deaf and blind, you must communicate by tapping signals on the back of their hand. You must communicate by touch.

And all of a sudden, the actions of Jesus did not seem so strange. He simply knew how to communicate in a way that was best for the person he was with. Jesus was willing to "speak" in whatever way was needed by the "listener."

At this, the man's ears were opened, his tongue was loosened and he began to speak plainly. (Mark 7:35)

We tend to communicate to others in the way that is most comfortable for us. But Christ communicated to others in whatever way was most useful to them.

- He used examples, stories, and object lessons.
- He preached, taught, and even smashed tables.
- He touched and poked and spat.
- He met each person at his or her point of need.

Perhaps we also need to set aside our pre-designed speeches and comfortable sermons and meet those around us where they are. To communicate to them in the way they need to hear. To touch and poke and perhaps even...give someone a big hug!

The Spell Checker

One of the greatest tools the computer has to offer is the Spell Checker. I almost did not make it out of third grade because of my spelling, so I am very grateful for the Spell Checker.

It haze the ability to look threw a litter and sea if their wood bee even won wrong world. Over the year, I half groan so confident with this suspect of the program, that I know longer knead to proof text me work. The niece think is the security I fill end knowing that the Spill Kicker will ever flail me nor lead me drown.

> "My hope is built on nothing less,
> Than Jesus' blood and righteousness.
> I shall not trust the sweetest frame,
> But wholly lean on Jesus Name."

It is amazing what we place our confidence in these days. We hope that a ton of metal will maneuver safely down a 14-foot strip of hardened rock at speeds many times faster than we can walk. We hope that a small plastic card will negotiate an agreement with a stubby metal box and convince the box to hand over hundreds of dollars, at any time of the day or night. We hope that a network of very loosely organized computers, chained together by marginally reliable phone lines, will deliver important messages to those we love, halfway around the world.

And the nice thing is that all of the examples work...most of the time. It is the times when the E-mail gets lost, the money machine is down, or the car careens out of control that we begin to understand why we need a solid, secure place in which to trust the safety of our very lives.

Nevertheless, God's solid foundation stands firm, sealed with this inscription: "The Lord knows those who are His." (2 Timothy 2:19)

And into this world of almost perfect production runs, Six-Sigma-error distributions, and nearly-flawless-mean-time-between-failure rates steps the example that, somewhere inside, we all desire. The One who is perfect. And what is more amazing is that He invites us to join Him in His perfection.

Therefore you are to be perfect, as your heavenly Father is perfect. (Matthew 5:48)

God,

We live in a world of almosts. It is almost perfect; it is almost flawless; it almost always works as planned. Almost... and we are grateful that You have placed us in a world that works so well, and You have given us the ability to perfect it all...up to a point. You have also placed within us the desire for the perfect. A desire for a system that we are absolutely certain will not fail. A desire to know You. And we are truly grateful that in Your hands we find that perfection. We find that certainty. We know that we know that we know that You are our God.

"On Christ the Solid Rock I stand,
All other ground is sinking sand,
All other ground is sinking sand."

CLICK AND DRAG

Because Microsoft Windows uses a Graphical User Interface, many of the tasks that were once done by typing commands can now be done using the mouse. We can click to get a menu of options, double-click to start a program, and click and drag to move things around. Clicking and dragging allows you to move an icon from one window to another, move a paragraph within a document, or move a file from one disk to another. All this is accomplished by simply pointing at the object we want to move, holding down the left mouse button, dragging the object to where we want it, and letting go.

What can be equally useful is that if you do not want to move these objects but would rather make a copy of them, you use the same click-and-drag procedure but hold down the Control key during the process. Files are quickly copied and graphics are exactly duplicated simply by using Control, click and drag.

I am glad that God did not use the Microsoft Windows environment when He created the world: "In the beginning, God created Adam, then He used the Control, click-and-drag function to replicate Adam to the utter most parts of the earth." There is something reassuring to know that I was *knitted* in my mother's womb rather than duplicated by a pointer and a mouse (Psalms 139:13).

The same God that shied away from using the Control, click-and-drag function in the creation process also avoids using the standard click-and-drag function in His day-to-day relationships with His creation. Rather than force us to believe in Him or impose His will on our lives and activities, God chooses to guide and direct us by speaking to us as a loving Father would talk with his children.

- When the world needed to hear His voice, He sent His Word.

- When He desires a missionary to travel across the world, He speaks to those who have made themselves available to Him.

- When someone desires to know who Christ is, He speaks to a believer's heart and encourages them to share about their relationship with Christ.

- As He daily seeks to draw us closer to His side, His still, small voice speaks to us to encourage and comfort and direct.

And your ears will hear a word behind you, "This is the way, walk in it," whenever you turn to the right or to the left. (Isaiah 30:21)

God will never click and drag us kicking and screaming into His will. He did not create us that way. He does not seek us that way. He will not guide us in that way. But instead, He uses His word, His Spirit, and His people to reveal the love that He has, the love that He is, and the love that He desires to share with each of us.

Rejoice today in the love of God. Draw close to Him, and He will draw close to you.

THE UNSAVED DOCUMENT

"**O**h no! Tell me this isn't happening. The document was all but done, then that quick blink of electricity. Now my computer is rebooting; and this has happened once too often for me to not know what I'm going to find when I start up my word processor again.

"What's that? Was the document saved?

"Well, not exactly. You see, I had been so busy that I really hadn't taken the time for that. The document had to be created, then the format changes had to be added; there was centering to be done, font changes to be made. I spell checked it and even ran the grammar check, because this was so important. And it was a great document; everything was done just right: It would have impressed everyone at the meeting.

"*Oh no. The meeting! It's only five minutes until…no wait, my watch is slow, the meeting is starting now. I hear the folks talking as they move toward the conference room. What will Mr. Johnson say when he finds out that…*

"Oh, Mr. Johnson…Hi,…the proposal?…Well, you see, it was all but finished…and it really looked good…and…

"No sir, I don't have it. No sir, it wasn't saved. Yes sir, I understand, sir…"

In a world that moves at a nano-second pace, in a culture that allows us every conceivable option (and some options that were better left unconceived), in a life filled with endless possibilities, it is a heartbreaking reality that everyday most of the folks around us move through life without ever focusing on the one thing that matters most. There are proposals to be written, movies to be seen, families to be loved, and countless other worthwhile activities to be undertaken. All the while, the God who created us and desires a relationship with us patiently calls and waits for our response.

For it is appointed for men to die once, and after this comes judgement. (Hebrews 9:27)

The same God who calls us will eventually judge us. He must. It is a part of His nature, and He will always be consistent with His nature. But His desire, more than anything, is that He will judge us through the sacrifice of Christ, pronounce us not guilty, and invite us into the celebration in His kingdom.

There is therefore now no condemnation for those who are in Christ Jesus. (Romans 8:1)

To equate a lost soul with a lost document would be to trivialize the importance of what our Savior has done for us. But to remember a lost friend every time we lose something we have worked on for several hours will, perhaps, help us keep focused on what is most important to Christ our Savior.

CLOSING A WINDOW

One of the nice things about the Windows environment is its ability to manage multiple activities. Several applications can run simultaneously, and it is easy to move from one to another. Two of the many options available for each window are to either close the window or to minimize it. In many ways, the outward appearance of these two options is very similar. Whether you close or minimize a window, it goes away from your current view and focus of attention. But, in actuality, these functions are very different.

When you minimize a window, you are really putting it on hold. The good news is that you can easily pick up what you were doing in that window, from right where you left off. The bad news is that even while the window is minimized, it is still using lots of system resources and is basically a distraction from the other things the computer should be working on.

In contrast, when you use the *close* function, the system takes the time necessary to put away the application that is no longer needed and frees up the resources to be devoted to other things.

Because He loves us, God is constantly working in our lives to change us and conform us to His image. These changes come in many ways and take many forms. One way is when He leads us to a point in our lives where He requires us to set aside an attitude or behavior that does not reflect His character—He calls us to close a window. But being the clever humans that we are, we think that the behavior may not really need to be closed; we can simply minimize it and achieve the same outward appearance.

We constantly minimize behaviors by telling ourselves that they are too small for a big God to worry about, or we convince ourselves that God will not replace them with something better and therefore we should keep them tucked away in the lower left corner of our life, where they are only a double-click away if we ever need them. We tell ourselves that if these actions are hidden from the rest of the world, what harm can they really be?

But even when minimized, these areas of our lives that God has called us to close can still use much of our resources. We lie to ourselves and to others, to keep them quiet. We constantly hear them in the back of our mind, calling for our attention. And when we try to focus on other things to which God has called us, we find these areas of our lives that we thought were minimized have pushed out the things that God wants to place in us.

And yet God continues to call us to close them. To take whatever time necessary to set aside what is not of Him, and put on the likeness of Christ.

… Let us also lay aside every encumbrance, and the sin which so easily entangles us, and let us run with endurance the race that is set before us. (Hebrews 12:1)

So what is God calling you to close in your life these days? What attitudes and behaviors has God shown you that no longer need to be minimized, but the time has come to close them for good. Closing a window in Windows is easy, just point and click; closing areas of our lives that may have been a part of who we were for many years but no longer reflect who we are in Christ, is much more difficult.

Fortunately, God has given us His Spirit to strengthen and guide us and His grace to sustain and forgive us as He daily conforms us to His image.

And for this purpose also I labor, striving according to His power, which mightily works within me." (Colossians 1:29)

Let this week be a week of closing windows in your life.

Hard Returns

This is not meant to be an age test, but here goes: How many of you have sat in front of a device where you typed for a little while, then a little bell went "ding" then you reached up and slapped a metal handle, causing the carriage to return to the start of the line? Yes, I see those hands! Most of us learned to type on these old typewriters (mine had *Royal* across the front) and have only recently moved into the world of word processors.

Remember the first time you typed on a word processor? When you reached the end of the line, there was no "ding." The cursor automatically moved back to the beginning of the next line, allowing you to continue typing without hitting the carriage return. This function of word processors is called the Automatic Word Wrap, and most people see it as a nice feature that saves us the hassle of hitting the Return key at the end of each line.

However, this is not simply a nice feature that you may or may not choose to use. Automatic Word Wrap is a feature that you must utilize in order for the word processor to work correctly. If you use the Return key at the end of each line, the word processor places a control code in the document called a *hard return*, which causes the word processor to start a new line anytime it reaches that point in the document. This does not cause problems until there are changes that need to be made to the document.

Perhaps the margins need to be smaller, a sentence added, or a word deleted. If the Automatic Word Wrap has been allowed to flow the words as it deems best, then the changes are easy to accomplish. But if the document is full of hard returns, almost any attempt to revise, reformat or introduce change into the document will be met with less-than-acceptable results.

Think for a moment about the principles that govern the way you live. What are the hard returns that you have placed in your life? What are those self-imposed absolutes that you have held on to all of your life, that make it almost impossible for God to effectively reformat your life?

"The sins of my past are too great, I could never be useful to God with that much stuff in my past."

"The sins of my present are too great, I could never overcome the sins I struggle with and be acceptable to God."

"Please, Lord, I have never been eloquent...I am slow of speech and slow of tongue." (Moses, Exodus 4:10)

In response to Moses' hard return, God simply responded, "Now then go, and I, even I, will be with your mouth and teach you what you are to say" (Exodus 4:12).

All documents need hard returns—at the end of a paragraph, after the salutation, etc. People need absolutes in their lives as well. The question is, Who puts them there? When we begin to substitute our absolutes for God's absolutes, we create a life that becomes rigid and constrained and limits God in His plans to revise us according to His will.

You can remove the extra hard returns in a document by simply deleting them. However, until they are all removed and the Automatic Word Wrap takes over completely, the document can look a little out of kilter. So be patient with yourself and with those around you, as God works in each of us to remove those things that keep Him from having complete control over every aspect of our lives.

MULTITASKING

Did you realize that Microsoft Word can undo not only the last mistake you made, but the last 100 mistakes you made? And that Excel starts with sixteen active spreadsheets as part of one book? Or that Microsoft Windows '95 offers "true" multitasking, which will allow the user to have an almost unlimited number of activities going on simultaneously? Isn't this exciting?!

I have often wondered about features such as these. I can barely remember the last couple of mistakes I have made, much less the last 100. If I have more than five or six spreadsheets related to any given project, I seriously consider simplifying the project. If I can barely keep focused on even one activity, what in the world makes me think I can keep up with multiple tasks? But yet I try to get as many projects going at the same time as I can. I double-book meetings; I hurry from one appointment to another. And the worst part of it is, as I participate in one activity, even if I enjoy it, my mind does not focus on that activity but is constantly preparing for my next commitment.

Then I stop and wonder what God thinks of all this. "But God, I must hurry. Many of these activities...well, at least some of these activities are for You. 'If I don't do them, who will?"

Be still and know that I am God. (Psalms 46:10)

"But we've been blessed with all these tools that can make us more productive for the kingdom! Our Bibles are electronic, our devotions arrive by E-mail, our lesson plans are downloaded from the Internet...."

Blessed is Mary, who desires to worship at My feet. (Luke 10:38–42)

"But it's the nature of our society. In a nano-second world, we've got to keep pace or be outpaced. Be a part of the solution and not part of the problem. Lead, follow, or get out of the way! How can we minister to those who don't know You, if we can't identify with what goes on in their everyday life?"

I've called you to be in the world, but not of it. (2 Corinthians 10:3)

And yet even as I hear the voice of God, my mind is already dwelling on all that I need to get done when I am finished writing and rereading this devotional.

Dear Father,
The world around me demands more and more from me everyday. My work, my family, even my church have my schedule so filled that I seldom have time for You. And my confession today is that even though I recognize what

is happening, I feel helpless to change it. Forgive me, and help me.

Focus me again on You. Place my relationship with You above all others. Give me the discipline and courage to turn aside from all that distracts me from You. Remind me again to seek You first. Amen.

WORDS OF WISDOM

ME: So, Dad, how was your weekend?

DAD: A little frustrating. I spent most of my time hassling with windows.

ME: Oh really, what kind of problems were you having?

DAD: Well, there were a couple of windows I couldn't get to open.

ME: Maybe you just weren't double-clicking quick enough or you weren't holding your hand steady.

DAD: [Confused] No, I just think someone did a sloppy job with the paint brush.

ME: Yes, that could cause problems. Maybe Mom opened the Paintbrush application and forgot she had it opened, then opened another copy and this caused an insufficient memory problem, which could keep you from opening other windows.

DAD: [Further confused] I don't think that was it. Mom was helping, but she was opening the paint can—not the paintbrush. And she may be old, but there's nothing wrong with her memory. Don't you think you should be a little more respectful...?

And when I came to you, brethren, I did not come with superiority of speech or of wisdom.... (1 Corinthians 2:1)

Me: So, neighbor, how was your weekend?

Neighbor: Busy. I had lots of work around the house to get done. Then I ran the kids all over the community for their activities. It seems like I just don't have enough time to get everything done. Sometimes it's downright depressing...

Me: Well, I spent most of my weekend working on stuff at my church. We had a bylaws committee meeting Friday night, kids party on Saturday, association meeting Saturday night. I got up early on Sunday to teach Sunday school; then in the service, the preacher spoke about the propitiation of sin. It was fascinating. Have you ever thought much about the propitiation of your sin?

Neighbor: Uh, well, sin has always sounded like an interesting proposition to me, but no, I haven't thought much about it.

Me: You should really begin to think about it. Once you understand the difference between sanctification and justification, life just seems to fall into place!

Neighbor: Uh, yea, just falls into place...

Me: And then you can really experience the excitement of being a Christian and having weekends like mine. Wouldn't you like to know more about that?

Neighbor: Well, I'm not certain...

Me: Well think about it. Maybe when I get back from the men's Bible study, you'll have some questions I can answer. See ya later. Bye!

My message and my preaching were not in persuasive words of wisdom, but in demonstration of the Spirit.... (1 Corinthians 2:4)

And the fruit of the Spirit is love, joy, peace, patience, kindness, goodness, faithfulness, gentleness, self-control.... (Galatians 5:22–23)

Query by Example

Select From "Some database whose name I can't remember."

Where Fieldnames = "I don't know. Just show me all of them."

Order By = "Whichever one you come to first"

Etc.

To create information from all the data stored in a database, one must learn how to correctly ask for the information. This may be by designing a report or perhaps, more frequently, by asking nicely in the form of a query: "Show me all the inventory items where the in-stock quantity is over 100." Queries allow you to cut through all the clutter and get specific answers to specific questions.

Databases have the distinction of being some of the most useful and some of the most complicated programs on the market today. Anytime I use a database and actually retrieve the information that I am looking for, I feel grateful.

Therefore, since we have so great a cloud of witnesses surrounding us, let us also lay aside every encumbrance, and the sin which so easily entangles us, and let us run with endurance the race that is set before us….(Hebrews 12:1)

Very few Christians live their life in anonymity. Our actions, our language, our Christlike nature, will eventually set us apart from a Christless society. As that begins to happen, we may receive open rejection or ridicule from the world around us, but it is more likely that we will become the focus of other people's queries. These queries may be issued directly to us, or they may happen as others watch what we do. The life we live is queried:

Select From "John R. Christian"
Where Fieldnames = "Dealing with Problems"
Order by = "First Reaction when the system goes down."
<or>
Select From "Doug K. Believer"
Where Fieldnames = "Dealing with Kids"
Order by = "Reaction to note from school regarding kid's conduct."

Specific queries seek specific, practical, useful answers. What that Christian believes about postmillennialism or Peter's preaching style during the first century may be accurate data, but it's useless information for someone who cannot relate to their teenager or who is burdened by the stress of their job.

A database has an easy life. We open the database, issue our queries, close the database, and allow it to sit unqueried until needed again. But a Christian's life is always available to be queried. The decisions we make, the reactions we have, the things we choose to spend our money on, and how we spend our time, all collect into a database that the world will constantly query for answers about life.

Sometimes these queries will be an effort to trap or humiliate. But usually they are desperate cries from a hopeless world, for specific answers to specific questions about how to cope with a difficult life.

What is exciting is that each day, by watching our lives, those around us can see a little more of Christ in us, until one day the queries will become a simple request: "Tell me how I can know this Jesus?"

For God, who said "Light shall shine out of darkness," is the One who has shone in our hearts to give the light of the knowledge of the glory of God in the face of Christ. (2 Corinthians 4:6)

Are You Sure?

"Are you sure you want to close Windows?"

"Are you sure you want to exit this application?"

"Are you sure you want to save these changes?"

And on and on it goes—the computer's never ceasing process of warning us about the actions we are taking.

One of the more common messages we get is: "Are you sure you want to delete this file?"

The message looks innocent enough, but in reality it is saying:

- "I know you just told me to delete this file, but have you really considered the consequences of this action?"

- "Have you thought about all the time invested in creating this file?"

- "Have you considered the permanence of your choice? Have you examined the impact on all the other files that are linked to this file?"

- "Do you fully understand the difficulty involved in restoring this file if necessary?"

- "Now tell me just one more time, are you really, really sure you want to delete this file?"

It seems, over time, that these messages become a pain in the bit, and we tend to click on the OK button without even reading them. We have seen the message so many times that we do not even listen to the warning anymore. That is until the one time we hit Delete, click on OK, then let out a gasp as we realize that it was not the file we wanted to delete, but rather it was our 12-month forecast that took two days to complete. We break out in a sweat and begin pounding on the computer, screaming, "Give it back! Give it back!" If only we would have listened to that simple, familiar warning.

The fear of the Lord is the beginning of knowledge; Fools despise wisdom and instruction. (Proverbs 1:7)

As we grow in Christ and begin to recognize His voice and the moving of His Spirit in our lives, we begin to realize that He is constantly providing us with the warnings that we need to avoid the influence of the adversary. It's that small tweak of our conscience, just after we think a harsh thought but before we say the harsh words: "Are you sure you want to say that?"

It's that awkward, uneasy feeling we get as we surf the channels and stop on something inappropriate: "Are you sure that this is what you should be feeding your mind?"

It's that sense of loss we feel when we leave for work just after arguing with our spouse: "Are you sure you want to leave this wound open all day?"

And just like the computer messages, we can let these "Spirit messages" become so routine that we overlook them, or treat them as unimportant. Then one day the harsh word spoken leaves a friend hurt or an unresolved argument leaves a marriage cold and empty.

But I say, walk by the Spirit, and you will not carry out the desire of the flesh. (Galatians 5:16)

Listen to the Spirit messages that God sends you today. Heed the warnings, follow the commands, take comfort in the encouragement. And look both ways before you delete that file!

TEMPORARY FILES

There is a subdirectory in Microsoft Windows called the TEMP directory. It is a directory that application programs use to create, manipulate, and delete files necessary for their operation. If everything runs smoothly, at the end of the day, before Windows goes home, it takes a quick look in the TEMP directory, encourages any remaining files along their way, then shuts the system down normally.

Things do not always run smoothly. Ocasionally something goes wrong in the system, things come to a screeching halt, and the system either crashes or simply refuses to work. When this happens, you can almost guarantee that there will be files left in the TEMP directory—files that once had a purpose but now just take up disk space. Files that were designed and created by an application to accomplish a job, but now they sit idle and useless, only to be forgotten or discarded when someone remembers to check the TEMP directory.

No one looked on you with pity or had compassion enough to do any of these things for you. Rather, you were thrown out into the open field, for on the day you were born you were despised. (Ezekiel 16:5)

68

He sits behind a thick glass window, holding the phone to his ear and talking about how he ended up in prison. He wears a plastic band around his left arm with his name and inmate number. His clothes do not fit well, and he sniffs often because it is cold in the cell. He was created in the image of God.

A fallen world can be tough on God's creations. When he was young, those around him supplied this man with drink and drugs, lied to him about right and wrong, and broadcast violence into his home until he thought it was OK for him to behave that way. They took God's creation and formed him into something that God never meant for him to be, someone that society itself no longer wants. And when his world crashed around him, he ended up in prison—an inmate, a TEMP file, created by a fallen world that is incapable of handling that which it has created. A TEMP file that once had a purpose but now is forgotten. A TEMP file that will be discarded when someone gets around to checking the TEMP directory. A man created in the image of God.

Are not five sparrows sold for two pennies? Yet not one of them is forgotten by God. (Luke 12:6)

Brothers, if someone is caught in a sin, you who are spiritual should restore him gently....(Galatians 6:1)

God,

I can't undo the evil that our society has done. I can't undo the sins that men commit. There are times when I don't even want to hear about the harm that man does against man.

But, God, don't let me forget those whom society has damaged and discarded. Those whose actions hide the image of their Creator that is in them. The ones who have sinned beyond belief but not beyond the cross. Place in me Your heart of compassion and kindness. Keep from me Your right to judge and condemn. Show me how to be Your voice of healing and restoration to the forgotten and discarded. Amen.

Multimedia Computing

I f you have not bought one, you have probably at least seen the new multimedia computers. They can do everything. They play full-motion video, answer the phone, display the faxes you receive, play Bach, and jump tall buildings in a single bound. They are funny, witty, sexy, and popular, and they can sing and dance. They are a natural product of our fast-paced society.

I have a 1906 copy of the Sears catalog. Just for fun, I looked up the hottest-selling children's toys for that year. They included a single-speed bike, a metal wheel that you rolled with a stick, and a variety of cute dolls. My, how times have changed!

Our need for constant stimulation has increased to the point that if our senses are not bombarded on a constant basis, we become bored, disinterested, and immediately start looking for other sources of stimulation (which is why I'm so dangerous with a remote control!).

As society progresses, the church has sought ways to respond and adapt its ministries. In some ways, our responses have been useful and necessary in reaching a changing world. In other ways, these changes have been a distraction, a source of confusion, and have resulted in a loss of identity for the modern church. For example:

- We want our music to be a tasteful blend of Mozart, Manhattan Transfer, and occasionally Motley Crew.

- The worship service needs to have the visual appeal of Hollywood but maintain the humility of Mother Theresa.

- We should experience the excitement of a football game within the beauty of the Sistine Chapel.

- We expect the humor of a comedy club, while providing answers on how to deal with AIDS, adultery, and loneliness.

- We are organized to the precision of a Broadway play, but feel we should create the informality and coziness of a visit to Grandma's.

- And oh, by the way, if we can keep all this to precisely an hour, that would help in planning other activities on our very busy Sunday schedules.

Somewhere in our desire to "become all things to all men," we have lost our focus on the simplicity and purity of the gospel. My fear is that in all the commotion, God has been overlooked, and He has found somewhere else to attend worship and to be worshipped.

Be Still, And Know that I Am God. (Psalm 46:10)

So how do we invite God back into our worship services? It won't happen with a new overhead projector, a better PA system, or even because we sing "Send the Old-Time Power." It won't happen for a congregation until God is invited into the individual worship of each person there. It won't happen until we set aside the schedules, the meetings, the "order of service," and replace all these with a renewed understanding that as we worship, we enter into the very presence of a Holy God. A God that demands and deserves, at the very least, our attention and acknowledgment, and at the very best, our worship and praise.

Today is Monday, which means that you have a whole week to forget this devotional thought before Sunday rolls around again. I ask that you would not let that happen. Begin today, perhaps even now, to lift a prayer to God. Ask forgiveness for all the distractions you have allowed in your life, and ask Him to bring you back into His presence. Make your only expectation of worship be that of encountering Him.

Upgrades

"But I must upgrade my computer. It has been almost nine months since the last time I added anything really neat!"

A reality of the computer industry is that technologies are in constant change. It seems that as soon as we buy something, it is obsolete and needs to be replaced by something faster, larger, or more complex. As I sit here in front of my "old" DOS-based 386, I wonder how much longer I will be able to survive before time has rendered my computer setup completely useless, and I will be "forced" to replace everything. (I hear there is something out there called Microsoft Windows that is really neat that I might want to try!)

But even as we clamor for the new, the exciting, the latest and greatest, we always place limitations on how much change we will accept in one dose:

"Yes, I want that new edition of my word processor, but don't make me learn any new commands or menu items."

"Of course I want that larger disk drive, but don't make me backup my old one and transfer all the data and disrupt my life."

"If it's not 'Plug and Play,' then I won't pay."

We continue this constant search to replace the old with the new, but with as little discomfort to our old life as possible.

...Since you laid aside the old self with its evil practices. (Colossians 3:9)

God must also deal with this same issue as He seeks to work in our lives. We call out to Him for help and salvation, which He willingly provides; but when He begins to make changes in our lives, we suddenly balk at what He is trying to do:

"Yes, I want that new Spirit of forgiveness and humility, but all my friends think my biting sarcasm is humorous and entertaining."

"Of course I want a larger capacity to love, but I really don't want to deal with those that are unlovely."

"Yes, I desire to let Your love show in my relationship with my spouse, but do You realize the amount of time and sacrifice that will take?"

We continue on and on, "Upgrade me, O Lord, but let me keep all my old ways as well...." We seek a cumulative salvation experience, asking God to add more and more good things to our same old spirit until it looks acceptable to Him and to the outside world.

But God's way is different:

For if any man be in Christ, He is a New Creature. Old things are passed away, behold, all things have become new. (2 Corinthians 5:17)

A new creature—a completely new being. Something that has never existed before. Not an upgrade to an old

75

system. Not a new chip in an old chassis. No, what God does in our lives is create a brand new being. Something that we cannot even imagine or expect or plan for ourselves.

Let's quit praying our new prayers: "Upgrade me, O Lord." And replace that with an old prayer: "Create in me a clean heart, O Lord" (Psalms 51:10).

Screen Savers

A long time ago, in a network far, far away, the average computer user worked with what was called a *dumb terminal*. I always wondered if this was a reflection on the user, the computer, or both. The dumb terminal I used was the ergonomically designed IBM 3278. I had this terminal for several years, and I began to notice, over time, that even after I had turned off the terminal, the main screen from the application I regularly used was still visible.

I was experiencing that dreaded condition called *burn-in*. This is caused when the exact same information is displayed on your screen for long periods of time, until the terminal actually has this information burned into the glass.

The advent of PCs changed all this. Because PCs are "intelligent," they can sense whether the user is using the computer or has fallen asleep—due to slow response time. Once a preset time limit has passed, the computer begins to generate some activity on the screen that will keep the glass from being permanently burned in. This feature is called the *screen saver*. Originally, the screen saver consisted of some randomly drawn lines or bouncing balls, but now we have everything from flying toasters, to Far Side cartoons, to personally designed messages for the rest of the office to read.

> O God, You are my God, earnestly I seek you; my soul thirsts for you, my body longs for you, in a dry and weary land where there is no water. (Psalms 63:1)

You may not have realized it, but the human mind comes with a built-in screen saver. It is that internal mechanism that keeps us from being able to focus on any one thing for more that a few minutes at a time.

• You sit down to read your Bible, then the next thing you know, your mind has wandered off to some randomly generated list of things to do or places to go.

• The pastor starts his sermon, and after the preset five-minute limit, your mind starts-up the I-wonder-what-all-these-maps-in-the-back-of-the-Bible-are-for screen saver.

• You commit yourself to a time of prayer, but your stomach starts to growl after the first few minutes.

So we frequently become distracted or lose our focus on Christ.

> Let your eyes look straight ahead, fix your gaze directly before you. (Proverbs 4:25)

> …That I may dwell in the house of the Lord all the days of my life, to gaze upon the beauty of the Lord and to seek Him in His temple. (Psalms 27:4)

My old 3278 eventually reached the point where all you could ever see was the first screen from the main application. The burn-in had become so complete that no other program, not even turning the terminal off, could erase the presence of that original screen.

I often wonder why I am constantly falling away from what Christ would have me do. Why can't I seem to feel confident about His will for my life? Why do I not seem to have His presence in all that I do? Perhaps it has to do with my innate screen savers, with my inability to focus on Christ and Christ alone. To gaze upon Him and not allow the distractions of my life to creep in and overcome my time with Him. I need to turn off these "screen savers" and allow the image of Christ to "burn-in" to my life.

Lord,

Help me focus. Help me to search for You, to worship You, to meditate upon You, to simply gaze upon You. Help me to set aside the busy-ness of my life, and rest in You.

Lord, replace my burn*out* with burn*in*. Amen.

Let Me Talk to the Guy
Who Designed This

The problem was with FORTRAN74, a version of FORTRAN that was long past its prime but was still holding its own in the small company where I worked. The program I had written compiled fine but would abend at the same place, with the same error every time.

After much research, I decided that the problem was not in my code but in the FORTRAN74 software itself. I made a call to the "Support Center" of the very large computer company that sold the software, and then the fun began. The very large company, keeping my best interests in mind, had developed a complex system to help analyze my problem, determine the causes, evaluate possible solutions, and recommend a course of action. Naively, I waded into this morass.

Three weeks later we were rapidly approaching the determine-the-causes stage of the process, and I was growing somewhat weary and frustrated. An off-handed comment revealed that FORTRAN74 had been written by some folk in a lab in Tucson. So without telling anyone, I quietly called the plant.

"Hi, I need to talk to someone in FORTRAN development."

"No problem, I'll transfer you."

"Hi, I've got this problem with FORTRAN74. Can you help me?"

"Oh sure, me and old Joe here were on the team that wrote that software. What can we do for you?"

About ten minutes later, my program was running fine, and I had gotten to know two very nice gentlemen in Fortran Development.

They exchanged the truth of God for a lie, and worshipped and served created things rather than the Creator…. (Romans 1:25)

Do you not know? Have you not heard? The Lord is the everlasting God, the Creator of the ends of the earth. He will not grow tired or weary, and his understanding no one can fathom. (Isaiah 40:28)

There is almost no problem too big or pain too deep that cannot be solved by a quick trip to a local bookstore. The "How To" section that was once filled with information on fixing auto carburetors is now dominated by books on fixing our hearts, minds, and emotions. Complex systems have been designed to heal our hurts and transform our dysfunctional past into a productive future. But the vast majority of these systems fail to do the one thing that would work the best: consult the Creator, the One who designed us from the ground up. The One who formed us in our mother's womb. The One who knows each of us as His child.

"Turn your eyes upon Jesus..."

The hurts we have are real. God said we would have them.

"Look full in His wonderful face..."

The past has not been kind. God said the sins of our fathers would carry from generation to generation.

"And the things of earth will grow strangely dim..."

But the solutions to these hurts should not be of our own making.

"In the light of His glory and grace."

The solutions are found in the Creator. In the light of His glory and grace.

Choosing Our Enemies

The notice I received was very urgent: "There is a virus going around that can destroy your system!!! It is called the Good Times virus and, if activated, it will delete all the files on your system!!! Please be on the lookout for this virus and be sure to delete it before it deletes you!"

The warning was a wake-up call, and I began immediately to scan my disk to see if I had somehow loaded this virus onto my system. Then I began to send notes to all my friends and neighbors to warn them of this virus. I even contemplated writing a batch file that would scan my In-Basket to look specifically for this file, so that it might never have the chance to get on my system.

There was just one problem: This virus never existed. There was no such virus as the Good Times virus. All of my efforts were unnecessary, even a waste of time. I was hunting for a problem that did not exist.

They will stumble over one another as though fleeing from the sword, even though no one is pursuing them. So you will not be able to stand before your enemies. (Leviticus 26:37)

The time was a few thousand years before Christ. The place was the wilderness outside of Egypt. The people were God's chosen people—the Israelites, those people closest to the heart of God. Those who had followed God out of the oppression of Egypt. Those who, on occasion, forgot all that God had done for them and began to do things their own way.

They were headed to the Promised Land, which was inhabited by people who had no intention of casually giving their land to whomever might stop by and tell them that God said they could have it. The enemies waiting for Israel were real and would prove to be a force with which to contend. But Israel had a little problem focusing on the most important issues.

It seems as if the real enemies were not enough, and Israel became preoccupied with enemies of its own creation. Enemies that did not exist, that Israel would fear, fight, or flee if they heard a rumor or saw a cloud of dust on the horizon. The end result was that Satan did not need to create real enemies to defeat Israel. They could create enough on their own to keep themselves preoccupied and distracted from what God would have them do.

Sometimes we give Satan too much credit. We lose our focus; we become frustrated in our jobs or struggle with our fears and insecurities. We focus our minds on potential struggles that never happen. We develop complex strategies to defend positions that are never questioned. We argue with unseen antagonists, rationalizing our behaviors and thoughts. We focus our energy fighting enemies that simply do not exist.

All the while, Satan is sitting back saying, "Boy, this is easier than I thought."

God's plan for the Israelites was simple:

But if they will confess their sins…I will remember my covenant with Jacob and my covenant with Isaac and my covenant with Abraham, and I will remember the land. …I will not reject them or abhor them…I am the LORD their God. (Leviticus 26:40, 42, 44)

His call was for them to return to Him, to focus on Him, to allow Him to direct their paths. His call is the same for us today: to return to Him, focus on Him, to allow Him to pick our enemies and provide us the means to defeat them.

God,

I cannot even count the number of times I am distracted each day. The battles I create and fight out of my own nature seem never-ending. I spend more and more time on things of less and less importance. Forgive me. Renew my mind. Choose my enemies. Secure the victories. Receive the glory and praise. Amen.

MAIL WAITING

Perhaps two of the most pleasant words in computer lingo are the words: Mail Waiting. Come on, admit it. When you log on to your system at work or your Internet connection at home, the first thing you look for is whether or not you have mail, isn't it? And aren't you just a little bit disappointed when you log on and there is no mail in your In-Basket? Congratulations, you're normal. Each of us enjoys receiving notes from across the Net. Receiving a note shows that someone else is thinking about you or they need and value your input on an issue, or they want to update you on what is happening with them, or they just want to say, "Hi." When mail is waiting, you know the sender desires to communicate specifically with you.

Thy word is a lamp unto my feet, and a light unto my path. (Psalms 119:105)

Over the years, God has communicated in many different ways, to many different people. There was the "still small voice" and the "burning bush." Remember the "voice from heaven" at Jesus' baptism? Remember when Balaam's don-

86

key spoke? And the list goes on and on. God uses His infinitely creative energy to communicate with His beloved creation.

But of all the ways that He has communicated with us, it is interesting that one of the most effective was also one of the simplest: He sent us a letter. A note, if you will. Written by God through men and sent across centuries under the watchful eye of the Holy Spirit. (Note: This watchful eye far exceeds any double-bit error protection system that we might ever dream up!)

A note from God. A note that says He is thinking about us—always. A note that says he desires our input back to Him—our worship, our praise, our prayers. A note to update us on issues, issues that never change, like love and life and trusting in Him. A note to just say, "Hello." Because sometimes we forget that He is there, and we wander off to struggle with life on our own.

Have you ever logged on to your system, saw the Mail Waiting indicator turned on, then just logged back off without bothering to check the mail, saying, "It's probably not important. I'll check it later, when I have more time." Or, "It's probably not meant for me. It was sent to the wrong ID and has no meaning or relevance to me." Or, "I already have too much going on; the last thing I need is another note making demands on my time."

God used thousands of people over thousands of years to send you a message like none you have ever read before or will ever read after. It is important. It is relevant. It is demanding.

On your desk at home, there is an old book from a heavenly Father about the things you are dealing with in your life even today. It has a Mail Waiting light on it. Check your mail.

CNTL-ALT-DEL

Control, Alt, Delete—three keys that are known to almost everyone who uses an IBM-compatible PC. The three keys that, one way or the other, will get you out of almost any situation you have encountered. Three keys that perform what is known as a *reboot*. Rebooting can be very useful:

- When the computer locks up and you cannot go on—reboot.

- When the computer gets lost performing a calculation and never returns—reboot.

- When the modem tries to disconnect, but the host computer just will not let go—reboot.

It is simple, efficient, easy to execute: CNTL-ALT-DEL, and the computer starts over.

But one thing I do: forgetting what lies behind and reaching forward to what lies ahead, I press on toward the goal for the prize of the upward call of Christ Jesus. (Philippians 3:13b–14)

Life is hard. We face life as a series of joys and struggles, hardships and triumphs, seasons of peace and war. We move through life learning, rejoicing, struggling, and growing closer to God as He directs our paths.

But sometimes things lock up. Sometimes life does not move forward. Sometimes all that we know comes crashing down around us, and life forces us to reboot. While this may be easy on a computer, it is devastating on a person.

A computer starts up again in a few seconds; for us it may take years.

A computer will lose a document or a few hours of work; for us, we might lose all we have and all we have known—all that has taken us a lifetime to build.

A computer clears the memory when it reboots. Our memories stay fresh and clear and painful.

Forgetting what lies behind….

"God, will I ever forget? The memories are too fresh, the struggle too recent, the hurt too real."

Reaching forward….

"Thanks, God, that there is a *forward*. To be honest, I don't even know what that *forward* will hold, but keep me reaching in that direction."

Press on….

"And in Your strength, I'll press on."

For the prize.

"Knowing that You are the prize. And that to be in Your calling is the highest place I can be. The most secure place I can be."

God,

Help me as I reboot. Steady me as I get up. Guide me as I start over. Amen.

INTERVIEW WITH A PROCESSOR

Now let me get this straight, you're a Processor?

"Yes, my given name is Intel 80486DX4-100, but my friends call me 486."

And in a few words, what is it you do for a living?

"Well, 'In a few words' is going to be a little tough. You see, I'm the most important part of the computer. You might be better off asking, 'What don't I do?' The complexity of my job is incredible. The demands on my time are constant. The interruptions never end. The…"

Yes, I see, but could you be a little more specific?

"My rule of thumb is: If it's going to be, it's up to me! When someone needs numbers added, I'm the one they call on. When a program needs information from the disk drive, I manage the request. When someone…"

But I thought some disk drives or CD-ROMs or monitors or other devices had their own processors built in?

"In some cases, that may be true to a limited extent, but I'm still the one everyone calls on to manage the whole process. You could call me the chairman of the processors."

I see. Now isn't your job made easier by others that are around you, like memory, for example?

"Yea, right. Have you ever tried to manage memory? The amount of my time I have to waste making up for memory deficiencies is incredible. I'm working on a way to replace memory altogether, but I don't have it quite worked out yet. By the way, if you're planning on talking to the other components as a part of this story, don't believe anything they say about me. You know how critical sub-systems can be."

Yes, so I've heard. Now tell me...Oh, hold on for a second. I think that was a knock at the door. Great news, the UPS guy just stopped by, and he dropped off something from your parents!

"My parents?"

Yes, it's from the Intel company, so it must be something from your family. Lets see. Oh neat! It must be a relative of yours. You look just alike. The only difference is that he has a tattoo on his back that says...let me see....I see it now...it says *Pentium!* Oh, and what's this? 'Instructions on How to Replace Your Old Processor...'

When He noticed how the guests picked the places of honor at the table, he told them this parable: "When someone invites you to a wedding feast, do not take the place of honor, for a person more distinguished will come and say to you. 'Give this man your seat.' Then, humiliated, you will have to take the least important place. But when you are invited, take the lowest place, so that when your host comes, he will say to you 'Friend, move up to a better place.' Then you will be honored in the presence of all your fellow guests." (Luke 14:7-10)

When Is a Delete, Not a Delete?

When you have some spare time this week, try this experiment: Take a large file and copy it from your hard disk to a diskette. Using a stopwatch, see how long it takes for the system to copy the file. Then delete the file you just copied. See how long the system takes to delete the file. Did you try it? If so, perhaps you are plagued by the same nagging question that people the world over have been asking for years: Why does the delete take about a tenth of the time the copy does?

I have done extensive research on this very question, and I think I have found the answer: The delete is not really a delete. That's right. When you delete a file from your computer, it does not really delete the file; it simply finds the file, then removes only the first letter of the file's name! The rest of the file is still there, but the computer no longer recognizes the information as useful. At some point in the future, it will store other data on top of this old file; but until that happens, the old file is really still on your computer.

These are the statues and the judgments which you shall carefully observe: You shall utterly destroy all the places where the nations whom you shall dispossess serve their gods, on the mountain and on the hills and under every green tree. And you shall tear down their altars and smash their sacred pillars and burn their wooden symbols with fire and you shall cut down the engraved images of their gods, and you shall obliterate their name from that place. (Deuteronomy 12:1–3)

Wow! When God deletes something, He really deletes it. There were no commands saying: "Go in and delete the first character, then the rest will fade away at some point in the future." No, the command was to *obliterate!* God is serious about deleting that which is opposed to Him.

If you keep reading the story in Deuteronomy, you begin to see why. Some of the Israelites thought God was a little too extreme on this point, and they disregarded His command. The nations they conquered were seen as a good source of slaves or wives or workers. But little by little, generation by generation, those that were spared the judgment of God became the destruction of God's people. Their beliefs infiltrated the beliefs of Israel. Their practices distracted the Israelites from God. By not removing this pagan influence, Israel was responsible for harboring and encouraging its own downfall.

God does not change. And while the command He gave to the Israelites a few thousand years ago may seem a little harsh today, it is still the command he gives us: Utterly destroy anything that takes the place of God on His throne in your life.

We are not just commanded to set it aside. We are not commanded to try not to think about it. We are not even

94

commanded to conquer it, then keep it around as a reminder of our victory. We are commanded to tear down, smash, and burn.

While it may get a little messy, perhaps this is a good week to look once again for those things that stand between us and God, take out our sword, and do some obliterating!

RESPONSE TIME

Years ago, the words *System X* were in the lower right-hand corner of the computer screen. More recently, there is a small symbol shaped like an hourglass where the pointer should be (which is cute, but still annoying). Both symbols are trying to communicate to me the same thing:

1. The computer is busy on other things at the moment.
2. The computer cannot be bothered with my request right now.
3. The computer (and therefore the user) is experiencing slow response time.

Yet they did not listen or pay attention; they were stiff-necked and would not listen or respond.... (Jeremiah 17:23)

Picture yourself as a computer in the hands of an all-powerful God. He has designed you from the chip up. He knows your inner workings. He knows your abilities and limitations. He has trained you, developed you, tested you, discipled you and now is ready to begin using you for His purposes. Imagine He issues a simple command to you and you respond with an hourglass:

- "Hold on for a minute God, I'm busy with other things, but I'll process that request as soon as I get a slice of time available."

- "Just a second God, I've got to check my programming to see if I can really accomplish that request. I may need more training, additional programming, or maybe even a seminary education."

- "I'll be right with you God, but I need to scan the Internet chat rooms to see how others will respond if I execute this command."

Meanwhile, an infinitely patient God waits, knowing that the sooner you respond, the sooner He can issue even more interesting, complex, and challenging commands, if you would just get off of square one.

But when God, who set me apart from birth and called me by His grace, was pleased to reveal His Son in me so that I might preach Him among the Gentiles...I went immediately....(Galatians 1:15–17)

The computer industry calls it *sub-second response time*, but what this means is that the computer returns the answer as soon as you issue the command. In the computer world, this is a good thing. In our world, this is a good thing as well:

- When a co-worker approaches you with a personal problem and you set aside your work to listen.

- When a teenager calls to play basketball and you turn off the TV and put on your sneakers.

- When the burned-out friend asks how you can keep your sanity in a crazy workday and you admit that by yourself you cannot, then take the time to explain how Christ can calm a turbulent life.

When the need arises and you respond immediately—without hesitation or distraction. The only pause is a pause to pray, thanking God for the opportunity. God has created you, trained you, empowered you. God has prepared you for the instructions He will give. Let today be a day of sub-second response time.

As Powerful as a PC Jr.

The computer field is full of phrases and sayings that have developed during the short but interesting Information Age. We refer to *bugs* in the system—a phrase coined when a live insect infiltrated one of the first computers and caused the system to fail. "Garbage in, garbage out" is used to emphasize the infallibility of the computer and the frequent fallibility of the user. When I worked for IBM, the much-maligned IBM PC Jr. became the generic name for any computer that was under powered and was quickly abandoned by the market. To be "as powerful as a PC Jr." was not the highest compliment a computer could be paid!

Then I will cut off Israel from the land which I have given them; and the house which I have consecrated for My name, I will cast out of My sight. So Israel will become a proverb and a byword among all peoples. (1 Kings 9:7)

"Israel will become a proverb. . . ." What an interesting way to describe the people of God. Yet God warned that if they were not faithful to Him, they would end up as only a proverb, a footnote in history; a slang phrase used by anyone making a joke about a nation that was under powered and abandoned.

As tragic as that would have been for Israel, the same warning is true for the people of God today. Perhaps you already hear the cliches from those around you:

- "The church is full of hypocrites. I would never go there."
- "Church is just for women and children."
- "All they ever talk about is me giving them my money."

And on and on until we run the risk of becoming a church that has become a proverb to the world around us. A church that is not in touch with the realities of a fast-paced, wealth-driven society that no longer perceives the need for a church, much less the God it represents. God's remedy for this is found in verse 6 of that same passage and is actually quite simple: "Follow Me."

When the world is so distracted by its own definitions of success that they write-off the church as an artifact from a bygone time: Follow Me.

When your coworkers cannot understand your insistence on honesty and truthfulness, even when it could cost the company money or you your job: Follow Me.

When society tries to arrange your schedule so that you no longer have any time left for your relationship with God: Follow Me.

And when the sins of a godless society begin to unravel society at the seams, and those around you look for a source of refuge and security, you can point them to the God that has carried you through and simply say: Follow me.

Then I will establish the throne of your kingdom over Israel forever, just as I promised... (1 Kings 9:5)

Be Ye Perfect,
Like a Pentium Processor

It was one of Intel's finest moments: the new Pentium processor—the fastest PC processor on the planet. The technology that would allow Intel to continue its dominance of the PC processor market into the twenty-first century. It seemed perfect except for one small problem. It was first noticed by a math professor who occasionally received wrong answers on long, complicated math problems. Then Intel itself acknowledged what they insisted was a very minor flaw in the chip design, which could cause a problem in the ninth decimal place in the rounding of a number.

On average, this problem would occur in one out of every nine billion calculations. To the average user, this meant one error in one spreadsheet once every twenty-seven years. Intel acknowledged the problem, downplayed the potential effects, emphasized the insignificance of their error, then sat back to watch the problem go away. The problem did indeed go away, but only after tens of thousands of complaints, millions of replaced chips, and a total cost of over $500 million dollars.

Be perfect, therefore, as your heavenly Father is perfect. (Matthew 5:48)

For a fun and exciting Sunday afternoon, turn off the football game, open your Bible to Leviticus, and peruse the Old Testament Law. You will learn which animals are OK to eat (although not necessarily desirable). You will learn how to style your hair, whom you can marry, how to offer a blood sacrifice, and when a particular sacrifice is appropriate.

You will also come to the realization that, try as you might, you will never live a life that is perfect according to the letter of the law.

Therefore no one will be declared righteous in His sight by observing the law; rather, through the law we become conscious of sin. (Romans 3:20)

Have you ever thought of the law this way? Many people see the law, especially the biblical rules, as an oppressive legal guideline that must be followed to the letter, even though we know it is not possible. But Paul saw the law as a reminder:

1. That no matter how we live or what we do, we will always be in need of a Savior.
2. Of what God expects: obedience.
3. Of what God provides: grace.

Intel paid a great price for breaking the laws of math, even though they tried to minimize their mistake. A great price was also paid for the laws we have broken, even though we often try to minimize the significance of our sins.

Therefore, there is now no condemnation for those who are in Christ Jesus, because through Christ Jesus the law of the Spirit of life sets me free from the law of sin and death. (Romans 8:1-2)

WAITING

The results of an extensive study have recently been published in a leading PC magazine. The study tested dozens of different processors (Intel, Motorola, etc.) at various speeds (75 to 300 megahertz) and in many different PC configurations. The results proved conclusively that every processor was identical with regard to one key characteristic: When there was no specific task at hand, when all the work had been completed, when there were no instructions to be processed, all computers waited at exactly the same speed.

In the morning, O Lord, You hear my voice; in the morning I lay my requests before you and wait in expectation.
(Psalms 5:3)

Waiting is the great equalizer in the Christian faith. Some Christians are skilled in particular areas of service, others have a wealth of experience they can use in ministry. Still others are gifted in a specific calling. But when God commands us to wait, we all wait at the same speed. And no matter how hard we try, it is impossible to speed up the process of waiting.

Perhaps this is because the process of waiting is not dependent on our activities, but is solely dependent on God—His timing, His plans, His activity.

But they soon forgot what He had done and did not wait for His counsel. (Psalms 106:13)

Of all the commands in the Christian experience, the call to wait can often be the hardest.

- "How can I wait when there are so many open positions at church?"
- "How can I wait when there is a lost world that needs to know?"
- "How can I wait when I get bored if I sit still too long?"
- "How can I wait when there are so many things that I want to do…?"

But still God calls us to wait.

- Wait for His movement in a lost world.
- Wait for the area of service that He will set apart for us.
- Wait quietly—long enough to hear His voice, instead of our own.
- Wait for each other, as God works in each of our lives, then in the life of our fellowship.

It is good to wait quietly for the salvation of the Lord. (Lamentations 3:26)

On what has God called you to wait these days? The direction of your job? A ministry at church? An opportunity to witness?

Allow God the time He desires to prepare you and others for the call He has in your life. Wait.

Connected to the Host

"**Y**OU HAVE LOST YOUR HOST CONNECTION!!!"
"HOST SESSION IS NOW BEING TERMINATED!!!"

"Aagghhh! But I can't do my job without the host. Don't you understand? All my resources are on the host system!" Years of acquired knowledge. Months of analysis. Days of final preparation. When I *stand alone*, I'm unable to accomplish my purpose.

"YOU HAVE LOST YOUR HOST CONNECTION!"
"HOST SESSION IS NOW BEING TERMINATED!"
"I GUESS YOU'RE JUST OUT OF LUCK!"

...His unspiritual mind puffs him up with idle notions. He has lost connection with the Head, from whom the whole body, supported and held together by its ligaments and sinews, grows as God causes it to grow. (Colossians 2:18b–19)

Have there been times in your walk with God when you found yourself disconnecting from Him? Your relationship with Him was distant, remote? Your times with Him were few and far between?

And did you realize how this lost connection affects so many areas of your life:

- Your communication with others is strained.
- Your conversations that were once "routed through the Host" are no longer filtered through His presence and have become bitter and angry.
- The resources you called upon for encouragement and assurance now sit idle, unused, and seemingly inaccessible.
- Your Bible is dusty; your Sunday school lesson is lost; your devotional books have been archived to tape.

It seems that even the normal routines of life become strained, difficult, and exhausting when we have lost that connection with our Lord. Fortunately, a few verses later, the writer of Colossians lets us know how to reconnect:

Set your mind on the things above, not on the things that are on earth. For you have died and your life is hidden with Christ in God. (Colossians 3:2–3)

Hidden with Christ in God. The connection with God is hidden in Christ from the earthly things that seek to disrupt that connection:

- Protected from the attacks of Satan.
- Sustained during our times of weakness.
- Kept active even when we lose sight of our need for the connection.

Christ has initiated a session with each of us. It is time for us to respond:

- Log on to things above.
- Re-establish your connection with the host.
- Be hidden in Christ today.

BEEEP! BEEEP! BEEEP! BEEEP!

Don't Bother the Teacher

The class I was teaching was "Introduction to Windows," and it was not uncommon to get many interesting questions from the new Windows users. The problem today was not the nature of the questions, but the quantity. One student in particular had an insatiable desire to learn and throughout the class was interrupting with questions. I have always said that there are no stupid questions, but this person was making me question that rule! As the class drew to a close, I dismissed the students and began to breathe a sigh of relief. While I was gathering my materials together, I noticed from the back of the classroom this same person making their way forward: "I just have a couple of more questions...."

The next day was Saturday, and I began to prepare my Sunday school lesson. The Scripture passage for the day was from Mark 5:35f., and it went like this: "While Jesus was still speaking, some men came from the house of Jairus, the synagogue ruler. 'Your daughter is dead,' they said. 'Why bother the teacher any more?'"

And I stopped. And my heart sank as I thought of my own actions as a teacher and how I had communicated the same thing to my students: "Don't bother the teacher any

108

more. Your questions are stupid. I'm tired. I don't have the time. I'd like to go home now. Don't bother the teacher." Then I compared my actions to those of Christ:

"Ignoring what they said, Jesus told the synagogue ruler, 'Don't be afraid, just believe.'" (5:36)

It seems that times have not changed much over the last few thousand years, and the voices of our day are still giving us the same advice: "Why bother the Teacher any more? We live in a post-modern society; The problems we face are different, unique, modern. Why bother the Teacher with these?" And while our question is asked in such a way as to seem kind and considerate of the Teacher's time, the truth is that we do not bother the Teacher because we do not believe He can help.

Christ's response to all of this is the same today: He ignores it. Then He turns to those who still have the courage to seek Him and says: "Don't be afraid, just believe." His advice is simple: Bother the Teacher.

When you have struggled with the same sin in your life for so long that you are certain He no longer wants to hear your confession: Bother the Teacher.

When the circumstances of life cause you to have questions about who God is and His concern for you: Bother the Teacher.

When the demands of life have made you so tired and irritable that you are sure no one would want to spend time with you: Bother the Teacher.

And the Teacher will take you in His arms and say: "Don't be afraid. I'm here with you, as I have always been. I will carry you through this. Just believe."

LETTING GO, HOLDING ON

T he directory was C:\BUSINESS\PROJS\LETTRS\ ARCHIVE, and the creation date was July 12, 1984. I opened the directory and looked over the filenames, trying to figure out what the files were. I could not remember. I tried to open one of the files but received the ASSOCIATED PROGRAM NOT FOUND message and realized that I had deleted the old word processor used to create these files several years ago. I pondered for a few seconds concerning what to do with these files, checked how much disk space they were taking up, then decided to just leave them there. I never delete anything.

I have a three-foot piece of electrical wire stored in my basement that I am sure I will find a use for someday. I have every book I ever read in college stored in a box in the attic. I know I will need to reference them at some point. I have the install disks for DOS 2.1.1, just in case....

You have let go of the commands of God and are holding on to the traditions of men. (Mark 7:8)

Life is a never-ending series of choices concerning letting go and holding on. For all people, regardless of religious beliefs, social levels, or personality types, each day

110

presents us with choices regarding what we will let go of and what we will hold on to. Who we are, what we believe about ourselves, and more importantly, what we believe about God, is reflected in these choices.

For those in the time of Christ, the traditions and the ways of men were of highest priority: "You are holding on to the traditions of men." And because it is impossible to choose both the way of God and the way of man, they chose the way of their own making. The way that was most comfortable to them. The way they could control.

Perhaps the life we live indicates that we have made the same choices:

- We let go of time with God to hold on to our hobbies, our social calendar, or our TV.
- We let go of time with our kids to hold on to one more deal made, report written, or program debugged.
- We let go of prayer and hold on to planning.
- We let go of trust and hold on to treasures.
- We let go of faith and hold on to "facts."
- We let go of the commands of God and hold on to the traditions that we have made.

Letting go and holding on. It sounds so simple; it is so difficult.

God,

Help me this week to let go of all that is not of You, all of the things that I have told myself that I need, all of my man-made and man-focused traditions that help me feel safe and secure, and all of the distractions that keep me from You. Help me to hold on to You, and to be comforted in the knowledge that You are holding on to me. Amen.

REMOTE PLACES

I looked for God in the whirlwind, but He was not there. I surfed for God on the Internet, and while I got many hits on the text, I still did not find His presence.

I wrote a macro that issued a query that searched for God in every book in the Library of Congress, but I did not find God. (I did, however, really irritate some nice folks at the Library of Congress.)

I even did a global search in my on-line concordance, but all I heard was a disk spinning.

So I shut down the system and took a long walk down a quiet, lonely trail. In the cool of the evening and the quietness of my heart, God found me.

When Jesus landed and saw a large crowd, he had compassion on them, because they were like sheep without a shepherd. So he began teaching them many things. By this time it was late in the day, so his disciples came to him. "This is a remote place, and it is already very late…. (Mark 6:34–35)

"This is a remote place…" How will the people be fed? Who will care for them? How will their needs be met?

"This is a remote place...." Where will we turn for help? "This is a remote place...." There is no one here, except Christ.

I have always had a fear of remote places. Being out in the dark, alone, with no way to help myself or get out of the situation. I am at my best when I am in control, in command, and in charge of the world around me. But sometimes God does not want my best, He wants me. And this is when I find Him leading me to a remote place. A place where the only thing I can count on is Christ. My only source of provision is Christ. My only hope for comfort is Christ.

Then he gave the loaves to His disciples to set before the people. He also divided the two fish among them all. They all ate and were satisfied.... (Mark 6:41–42)

God,

It seems like I am never satisfied. I develop plans and implement strategies. I set goals and devise programs. I surround myself with the best people and programs I can find, yet I remain unsatisfied. Perhaps it is time for me to follow You to a remote place, where all I need will be found in all You are. Where I can be with You, and be satisfied. Amen.

Inside Job

My need for change was obvious. I had been using my DOS-based 386-SX computer for almost five years; and in computer years, that is an eternity. I set my mind toward accomplishing this change, and it was easier than I thought. I was able to change my entire system with three simple actions:

1. I found a computer magazine that had an advertisement for an Intel Pentium system. I cut out the little logo that said INTEL PENTIUM PRO INSIDE, and I taped this logo over the old model number on my PC.

2. I found a training manual for Windows '95 that had a picture of the main screen. I cut out this picture and glued it to my monitor.

3. I went to the pet store and bought a small mouse and placed it in a cage next to my computer.

And just like that, I had a new computer with all the latest bells and whistles! (I also ran speaker wire from my stereo into my A drive so that I could use the new CDs, but this was more complicated than I want to get into right now.)

Blind Pharisee! First clean the inside of the cup and dish, and then the outside also will be clean. (Matthew 23:26)

Picture in your mind the coffee cup you keep at work—the one you use for your morning cup of coffee that displays your company logo or some clever joke. Now picture how that cup would look if you never washed it. (For some of you this won't be too difficult.)

Now you know what a Pharisee looks like to God. And you also know what we look like to God when we try to clean up our act by changing our habits or making resolutions or trying the latest *How to Be an Incredible Person* book. We slap on new labels, glue on new attitudes, or buy clever accessories, but God still sees our heart.

Richard Foster put it this way in his book, *Celebration of Discipline:* "The needed change within us is God's work, not ours. The demand is for an inside job, and only God can work from the inside."

Only God can work from the inside, but it is still our decision whether we will allow this or not. We must decide if we will give the Creator free reign in our inner-most parts. We must choose to set aside our outward attempts at change and allow Him to work His change from the inside out.

The choice is ours. But if we insist on doing it our way, we will probably continue running at the same old speed, looking at life through the same old monitor, and having to deal with small rodents cluttering up our workspace. Trust me, I know!

COLORS

The program I was using was a standard spreadsheet program. I had completed the mathematical formulas and all that remained was to make the spreadsheet look good. I did some simple formatting, changed a few fonts, added some dollar signs, and then decided to add a background color.

After my first attempt, I realized that the color would be too dark and the data would be hard to read. My second attempt left the spreadsheet with a washed-out look. I finally decided not to bother, and I changed the color back to white. But something was still wrong. I tried again to paint the background white, but instead of a default spreadsheet, I got this bright-white look behind my data. A look at the help menu solved my problem. If I wanted to get back to the way the spreadsheet was originally designed, I could not simply paint it white. I had to remove all the colors, including white. I had to choose the color *none*.

...You are like whitewashed tombs, which look beautiful on the outside but on the inside are full of dead men's bones and everything unclean. In the same way, on the outside you appear to people as righteous but on the inside you are full of hypocrisy and wickedness. (Matthew 23:27b–28)

So what is your favorite color? For the religious leaders of Jesus' day, it was white. White communicated goodness, religiousness, piety, and perhaps a little bit of superiority as well. But that was then and this is now, and we are much more sophisticated in our color coordination:

- Red shows our power and authority.
- Green conveys our concern for the earth.
- Metal colors communicate rebellion.

And the list goes on and on, the right color for the right mood or status or politically correct idea.

Christ was not impressed by colors in His day. He saw straight through the whitewashing the leaders applied to their lives and right into their hearts. He sees straight through our colors as well. All of our attempts to whitewash our actions, our attempts to justify our behavior in the name of expediency or commerce or even religion, are useless under the steady gaze of Christ. A gaze that sees our sin for what it is, and causes our God to see red—blood red. And His red blood is the only color that we will ever need, the only color that can wash us white as snow.

Are you washed, in the Blood.
In the soul cleansing Blood of the Lamb.
Are your garments spotless, are they white as snow,
Are you washed in the Blood of the Lamb!

MOTHERBOARDS

It looked as if a package of fireworks had gone off inside my pastor's computer. There were pieces of computer all over the room. Disk drives here, memory chips there, over in the corner was a keyboard; the mouse hung lifelessly over the edge of the table. It was a sight that could strike fear into the heart of any computer user. Sitting right in the middle of all this chaos was the chairman of the deacons. And instead of fear, his face had a look of childlike delight and eager anticipation. He had decided to upgrade the motherboard!

The motherboard is the part of the computer that holds the whole thing together. All the components use the motherboard to do their jobs. She solves the conflicts, manages the resources, provides a home for the main components, and keeps the entire operation running smoothly. Every computer needs a motherboard. Things just will not work without one.

But after hearing of Him, a woman whose little daughter had an unclean spirit, immediately came and fell at His feet. (Mark 7:25)

The scene was in a small town on the coast of the Mediterranean Sea. The people involved included Jesus and a woman whose daughter needed Jesus' help. The daughter could not come to Jesus herself. Perhaps she was too young; perhaps she was too ill; perhaps she did not know she needed to see Jesus…but the mother knew. And the love she had for her daughter caused her to set aside any thought about herself, and act on behalf of her child.

In a strange town, surrounded by men of a different race and of a different religion, in the midst of big burly fishermen and sinister looking tax collectors, she approached the only one she believed could help. She turned to Jesus. Not for herself but for her child. And because of her faith, Jesus healed her daughter.

Being a mom means many things. It means resolving conflicts and managing households and keeping everything running smoothly. It means being the one, sometimes the only one, who is holding things together. But it also means knowing there are times when what your child needs, more than you, is your faith in Christ. It means knowing that there may come a time when those you love feel unable to approach Christ. And they need a mom to do that for them.

Perhaps there are those around you today that need a mom. They need one whose faith is a little stronger than their own. They need someone to pray for them, to hold them, to share their needs with Christ. Let today be a day of reaching out to those in need. A day of praying for those who feel like they can't pray for themselves. A day of being a spiritual mom to those around you.

And going back to her home, she found the child lying on the bed, the demon having departed. (Mark 7:30)

119

My Computer

I had saved my money for months, researched the decision for weeks, fretted for days, then finally took the step to buy a new computer. It was the fastest and best I could afford, and when it finally arrived I was like a child at Christmas. I hooked it all up, turned on the power, and when Windows '95 finished booting up, I saw nothing more than a blank screen with a small icon in the upper left corner that said My Computer. A smile slowly etched across my face and a sense of pride and satisfaction came over me as I said, "Yes, this is my computer! I own this one. I can't wait to see all that my computer can do!"

Say to the owner of the house he enters, "The Teacher asks: Where is My guest room...?" (Mark 14:14)

The Teacher was Jesus; the time was near the Jewish Passover celebration; the place was Jerusalem, and Jesus was looking for a place to celebrate this festival with His disciples. He sent a disciple ahead to find the right location and to ask an interesting question: Where is My room? Not: Where is a room? Or, Where is the room? Or, Would you spare a room? But rather, Where is My room? Where is the

120

room that is set aside specifically for Me? Where is the room that is intended for My purposes? Where is the room that is furnished and ready for My holy moment? Where is My guest room?

Christ is still asking the same question: "Where is My room?" And in the home of your life, how might you answer Him?

- "Your room is the foyer, where all who enter will know You are present in this home."

- "Your room is the kitchen, for You are our provision and our source of strength."

- "Your room is the family room, where You are the center of our family, our fellowship, our friendships, and our entertainment."

- "Your room is the bedroom, where we rest secure in the knowledge of your protection."

- "Your room is the study, for all knowledge begins and ends in You."

- "Your room is the tool closet, for all my works of service are in vain if they do not start with You."

- "Your room is even the deck out back, where You can watch Your sunset over Your creation and remind us each day that all You have created is indeed very good."

So when Christ asks you, "Where is My room?" which of these rooms will you give Him? It's a hard decision. Why not make it easy on yourself and give Him all of them?

121

Unrecoverable Errors

You have experienced a GENERAL PROTECTION FAULT at address 0000:EA34:002E. This is a bad thing! Would you like to CLOSE or IGNORE? (And by the way, the IGNORE doesn't really work!)

Have you ever received a message like this? I hate this message! I paid $2000.00 for this computer, $579.99 for this software, $22.79 for the manual to learn how to use the whole thing, and the best it can do is a General Protection Fault? I'm unimpressed. You would think that with all of the work it took to design the microprocessor, along with all of the hours to program the software, they would have created a system that could run smoothly. With all it has going for it, you would think that the system would be perfect.

The steps of a man are established by the Lord; And He delights in his way. (Psalms 37:23)

King David, who wrote the words above, was known for many things: his wisdom and leadership, his love for God, his poetry and songs, his adultery and murder, etc.

David was a man whose steps, for the most part, were established by the Lord. But as soon as David wrote the words above, he followed them with these words:

When he falls.…(Psalms 37:24)

It seems like a contradiction. If the Lord establishes a man's steps, when would he ever fall? If a man's actions are in accordance with God's will, when would he ever stumble? If a computer program is so well written, why get a General Protection Fault?

The answer is the reality of life here on earth: As long as we are on this side of heaven, we will always be human. And so the verse does not say *"If he falls,"* but *"When he falls, he shall not be hurled headlong.…"*

And even though God specifically says we will *"not be hurled headlong,"* there are many Christians lying face down in their tracks, thinking they will never be able to get back up, thinking they have failed God, thinking they have committed an unrecoverable error that they can neither close or ignore. While all along, God would say, the verse isn't over yet, keep reading, "Because the Lord is the One who holds his hand."

The God who guides our steps is the same God who holds our hand when we fall. The same God who steadies us when we stumble. The same God who sets us on our way again. The same God who will establish, and re-establish our steps all the days of our lives.

Hold to His hand, to God's unchanging hand.
Build your hopes on things eternal.
Hold to God's unchanging hand.

FOLLOWING THE RULES

Then the chief of the programmers came to Jesus with a complete and documented list of all grievances. They were accusing Jesus of many inappropriate practices:

1. Incorrect use of the programming languages. This included not using the commands the way they were suppose to be used and interpreting them in ways the chief programmers did not like. It took hundreds of years to take the simple commands and expand them into the complex commands they are today. These commands should be strictly adhered to.

2. Not washing His hands before He programmed. The programmer's handbook, which is an essential addition to the basic rules of programming, requires that a programmer wash his hands in a specific and detailed manner before touching the keyboard. Any variation from this rule would simply be inappropriate as well as unsanitary.

3. Programming on Sunday. It does not matter that you might be programming for no charge or for the good of a helpless person in need of care. You should never

program on Sunday, but if you do program on Sunday, you should at least charge double-time plus per-diem.

4. Programming with tax collectors and prostitutes. The Programmer's Guild has worked long and hard to insulate itself from persons that might damage the reputations of the programmers and erode the basic salary structure. There are specific people with whom the programmers can associate, and this social structure must be maintained.

And Jesus responded by saying, "Woe to you, you evil programmers. You walk through the cubicles of the user groups carrying large, heavy manuals in an effort to look wise and superior, but yet you steal code off the Internet to develop your own webpages."

"You screen calls and dump work on junior programmers and spend most of the day playing Solitaire, FreeCell, or worst yet, Minesweeper."

"You break the rules you quote, you ignore the people you are hired to serve, and you have a drawer at home full of pens and pencils you have stolen from the company."

And the programmers gasped in horror, because they wondered how he knew about the pens and pencils. Then they fled to their cubicles and plotted to create a virus that would stop Jesus before the user groups heard His words of truth, which would put them out of a job.

And they tie up heavy loads, and lay them on men's shoulders; but they themselves are unwilling to move them with so much as a finger. But they do all their deeds to be noticed by men... (Matthew 23:4–5)

But the greatest among you shall be your servant. (23:11)

125

Things That Don't Compute

There are three...no, four things that don't add up:

1. A Lotus formula without an ampersand sign.
2. An offering without a smile.
3. An Excel formula without an equal sign.
4. A budget without a tithe.

There are four...no, five things that don't work well at all:

1. Windows '95 on 4 meg of memory.
2. A leader without a prayer life.
3. A 300-baud modem.
4. A people without a vision.
5. America On-Line at 7:00 in the evening.

There are four things that simply don't compute:

1. My FORTRAN programs.
2. A church with a closed heart.
3. One of the original Pentium chips.
4. A person that will not forgive.

There are four things that are too wonderful, five that I do not understand:

1. The way of an E-mail across the Internet.
2. The work of God in the life of a tired and weary sinner.
3. The way of the mouse on the pad.
4. Unconditional love.
5. And how they came up with all those error statements that make no sense to anyone that doesn't have a Ph.D. in computer science.

Under three things the earth quakes, and under four it cannot bear up:

1. A lost file that was not backed up.
2. An undisciplined man surfing the Internet.
3. A computer, when it supplants a wife.
4. An unprepared church at the door of the twenty-first century.

I have not learned wisdom, but I have knowledge of the Holy One. (Proverbs 30:3)

(Very loosely based on Proverbs 30, with apologies to King Solomon.)

To find out more about Modem Ministries and read additional devotionals by Ellis Bush, visit our Website:

There are several ways to order additional copies of

Did Jesus Use A Modem At The Sermon On The Mount?

1. From the Author, Ellis Bush (ellisbush@compuserve.com) Send $11.00 per book to:

   Ellis Bush
   185 Newberry Commons, #321
   Etters, PA 17319-9362

   Note: The $11.00 includes shipping and handling. Check the Website for information on quantity discounts and the additional shipping charges for International Orders.

2. Order from WinePress Publishing by using their 1-800 number:

   # 1-800-917-BOOK

   or their Website: www.winepresspub.com

   Note: The cost will be $9.95 plus their shipping and handling charges, and they do accept most major credit cards.

3. For Bookstores or Organizations that desire to purchase in quantity, please contact Ellis Bush electronically or by snail mail at the address listed above. Or contact WinePress Publishing at 1-800-326-4674